MARTIAL ARTS HISTORY MUSEUM
HALL OF FAME

VOLUME 4: 2011 - 2014

Making an Impact

MARTIAL ARTS HISTORY MUSEUM
HALL OF FAME

VOLUME 4: 2011 - 2014

Making an Impact

AUTHORED BY
Museum President Michael Matsuda

EDITED BY
Karen Matsuda

FOREWORD DEDICATION TO
John Corcoran

DISCLAIMER

Please note that the publisher and author of this book are NOT RESPONSIBLE in any manner whatsoever for any injury which may occur by reading and/or following the information herein.

The photographs or information in this book cannot be duplicated, copied or referenced for any purpose without expressed, written permission from the author or the Martial Arts History Museum.

Copyright 2022 by Michael Matsuda. All rights reserved. Published in 2022. Printed in the United States of America.

DEDICATION

To my wife Karen, who believed in me and made this museum a reality. To my boy Sparky, who brought me such joy; I miss him everyday. But mostly to my Lord who makes all things possible.
－－ *Michael Matsuda*

ACKNOWLEDGEMENTS

Thanks goes to all those who believe
in me and believe in the importance of the
museum. We have a place where our history,
our memories, our accomplishments and our
legacy won't be forgotten.

A special thanks to Eric the Trainer
for all your efforts!

JOHN CORCORAN (2004) POSING FOR A SHOT OF HIM AND HIS "FUNAKOSHI AWARD" AS HE REMARKED, "THIS IS THE ONLY AWARD I EVER WON THAT ACTUALLY MEANS SOMETHING."

DEDICATED TO MY FRIEND, JOHN CORCORAN
Foreword

"This award was a symphony in the soundtrack of my life,"
— *John Corcoran*

I dedicate this forward to a great man and a dear friend, John Corcoran.

I had the honor of meeting John back in the 1980s, and through his inspiration, he encouraged me to become a writer.

Let me point this out: John was a great writer. He was the Babe Ruth of writing. In all my years as a journalist, I have never met someone so talented as a writer. If writings could be hung in museums, his work would be the Mona Lisa.

JOHN CORCORAN
2004 FUNAKOSHI AWARD WINNER

I, however, am just an ordinary writer. My grammar is ok, my style is so-so, but I'm great at press releases. Oh yes, I've written many books and articles, but I could never place myself even close to John.

With that said, my dear friend, John, passed away two years ago. He was

not doing well, and he knew his time was near. In our last conversation, he said he really wanted to attend Dragonfest that year. He said, "All my friends are at Dragonfest, and I want to see them. Afterward, I'm treating you to a steak dinner." Sadly, John passed shortly before the event.

John's biography and his contributions can be found in one of the Hall of Fame volume series, but I wanted to make this special forward to pay my respect.

The one thing that I truly would like to say about John, is that he has always been there for me. I remember so many times when John called me up and said, "Michael, what can I do to help the museum. How can I offer my services to ensure our history?"

Without any discussion of compensation, John Corcoran volunteered his time to provide the museum with historical information, straighten out our facts, clarify our data, and ensure everything the museum did was as accurate as possible.

It was John who would call me on the phone and discuss martial arts history and what he thought should be part of the museum.

I recall John saying to me nearly 15 years ago, "Michael, this museum better work because I'm going to do everything I can to help you. Don't leave me hanging."

John had a great soul. He was always laughing, enjoying life and being with other people.

When I needed something right away, John would get it for me. When he needed

something from me, I got it to him as quickly as possible.

John was a man who loved words. He told me one time that the new editors of the magazine would critize him, and had no respect for him. Obviously, they didn't know what kind of man John was. He was there in the trenches, he was there when history was being made. He was part of history.

. John donated a significant amount every month to the museum for years until his passing.

I was honored to have John Corcoran write the forward to the museum's Hall of Fame books, and not once did he ask for his name to be mentioned in the credits.

John was more than a great man, more than a great writer, and more than a great martial artist; he was my friend, and I genuinely miss his guidance.

To you, John!

—— THIS BOOK HIGHLIGHTS THE CONTRIBUTIONS OF ——

THE MARTIAL ARTS HISTORY MUSEUM HALL OF FAME INDUCTEES

VOLUME 4: 2011 - 2014

Making an Impact

THE MARTIAL ARTS HISTORY MUSEUM
HALL OF FAME

1999
AL DACASCOS
FUMIO DEMURA
BONG SOO HAN
TAK KUBOTA
BRUCE LEE
TOSHIRO MIFUNE
CHUCK NORRIS
JHOON RHEE
CYNTHIA ROTHROCK
BENNY URQUIDEZ

2000
GICHON FUNAKOSHI
WONG FEI HUNG
DAN INOSANTO
GENE LEBELL
YIP MAN
MAS OYAMA
EDMUND PARKER
MORIHEI UESHIBA
BILL WALLACE
TADASHI YAMASHITA

2001
RICHARD BUSTILLO
JACKIE CHAN
HELIO GRACIE
HAENG UNG LEE
JOE LEWIS
DON WILSON
TED WONG
YAU-CHUN WONG
JIMMY H. WOO
YOSHIAKI YAMASHITA

2002
RALPH CASTRO
HEE IL CHO
JIGORO KANO
ERIC LEE
JOO BANG LEE
JAMES LEW
ERNIE REYES
KAREN SHEPERD
ROBERT TRIAS
DOUGLAS WONG
FUNAKOSHI AWARD
NANCY KWAN

2003
BILLY BLANKS
HOWARD JACKSON
KATHY LONG
GERALD OKAMURA
CECIL PEOPLES
CHAN PUI
LILLY RODRIGUEZ
BILL RYUSAKI
DONNIE WILLIAMS
DOC FAI WONG
FUNAKOSHI AWARD
ART CAMACHO

2004
SONNY CHIBA
JOE CORLEY
STEPHEN HAYES
SHO KOSUGI
MICHAEL MATSUDA
HIDY OCHIAI
STEVEN SEAGAL
KOU SZE
ARNOLD URQUIDEZ
BYONG YU
FUNAKOSHI AWARD
JOHN CORCORAN

2005
GRACIELA CASILLAS
S. HENRY CHO
MICHAEL DEPASQUALE
JIM HARRISON
TED LUCAYLUCAY
CHUCK MERRIMAN
CARRIE OGAWA-WONG
BLINKY RODRIGUEZ
STEVE SANDERS
ALLEN STEEN
FUNAKOSHI AWARD
JOE HYAMS

2006
CACOY CANETE
LEO FONG
WALLY JAY
BUCK SAM KONG
BRENDAN LAI
LILY LAU
MIYAMOTO MUSASHI
TOSHISHIRO OBATA
ARK YUEY WONG
WEN MEI YU
FUNAKOSHI AWARD
FARIBORZ AZHAKH

2007
EMILIO BRUNO
YONG SUL CHOI
ROYCE GRACIE
SOL KAIHEWALU
SHINTARO KATSU
BEN LARGUSA
ARLENE LIMAS
RICHARD REED
MIKE SWAIN
AKEBONO TARO
FUNAKOSHI AWARD
RICHARD ALARCON

2008
ANTHONY CHAN
JEFF CHAN
HONG HI CHOI
RANDY COUTURE
LINDA DENLEY
MICHAEL DILLARD
MAKI MAYAHARA
HIDETAKA NISHIYAMA
LUCIA RIJKER
TAT MAU WONG
FUNAKOSHI AWARD
RAFAEL KOSCHE

THE MARTIAL ARTS HISTORY MUSEUM
HALL OF FAME

2009	**2010**	**2011**	**2012**	**2013**
ANGEL CABALES	JIM ARVANITIS	MIKE CHAT	JUN CHONG	LAU BUN
RORION GRACIE	WILLIAM K.S. CHOW	ADRIANO D. EMPERADO	KEIKO FUKUDA	PETER CUNNINGHAM
JOSEPH JENNINGS	PAUL DE THOUARS	KEE HWANG	KAYLA HARRISON	ALAN GOLDBERG
TAIHO KOKI	ANDREW FREUND	JI HAN JAE	TAEJOON LEE	JAMES HONG
CUNG LE	DANA HEE	TOM LAUGHLIN	TSUTOMU OHSHIMA	MAKO IWAMATSU
BOW SIM MARK	JOHN MCCARTHY	AL NOVAK	KEN SHAMROCK	DAVE JOHNSON
BRUCE TEGNER	TARAO MORI	DAN SEVERN	ALEXANDER FU SHENG	RICHARD RABAGO
KARYN TURNER	REMY A. PRESAS	LEUNG SHUM	NAI KHANOM TOM	FELIX ROILES
ANGI UEZU	CHAI SIRISUTE	IN HYUK SUH	ROGER TUNG	MARK SHUEY
DANA WHITE	HAYASHIZAKI SHIGENOBU	CARL TOTTON	KAM YUEN	TINO TUIOLOSEGA
FUNAKOSHI AWARD	*FUNAKOSHI AWARD*	*FUNAKOSHI AWARD*	*FUNAKOSHI AWARD*	*FUNAKOSHI AWARD*
AKIRA KUROSAWA	ED PARKER JR.	KAREN MATSUDA	MICHAEL MATSUDA	ANNA MAY WONG

2014	**2015**	**2016**	**2017**	**2018**
DAVID CARRADINE	J. PAT BURLESON	MIKE ANDERSON	MALIA BERNAL	JAMES BREGMAN
SAU CHUNG CHAN	GINA CARANO	BUAKAW BANCHAMEK	LEO T. GAJE	RON VAN CLIEF
JOHN LEM	GEORGE CHUNG	HAWKINS CHEUNG	TONY JAA	KIM KAHANA
ALBERT LEONG	DONN F. DRAEGER	WILLIAM CHEUNG	TI LUNG	LO LEIH
CHARLES LEWIS	PAT JOHNSON	DAN IVAN	MOSES POWELL	CHOJUN MIYAGI
CHUCK LIDDELL	PAT MORITA	MITSUYO MAEDA	PETER URBAN	NG MUI
JEFF SMITH	STEVEN LOPEZ	LAU FAT MAN	MITO UYEHARA	HAYWARD NISHIOKA
CHUCK SULLIVAN	FRANK SHAMROCK	MICHELLE MANU	CHERYL WHEELER	HENRY OKAZAKI
CHEN KUAN TAI	GOGEN YAMAGUCHI	MANNY PACQUIAO	MICHAEL JAI WHITE	ROBERT REDFEATHER
JAMES WING WOO	KEITH YATES	ELVIS PRESLEY	CURTIS WONG	RONDA ROUSEY
FUNAKOSHI AWARD	*FUNAKOSHI AWARD*	*FUNAKOSHI AWARD*	*FUNAKOSHI AWARD*	*FUNAKOSHI AWARD*
OSAMU TEZUKA	BILL WEBBER	ED IKUTA	JOAN KOSCHE	RUN RUN SHAW

THE MARTIAL ARTS HISTORY MUSEUM
HALL OF FAME

2019	2020
CHIBANA CHOSEN	DENNIS ALEXIO
DEMETRIUS HAVANAS	H.C. HWANG
DANIEL LEE	HIROZAKU KANAZAWA
ISAO TAKAHASHI	SAMUEL KWOK
FLORENDO VISITACION	GORDON LIU
KEITH VITALI	TITO ORTIZ
AL WEISS	STUART QUAN
DR. JWING-MING YANG	CHRISTINE BANNON-RODRIGUES
LU CHAN YANG	THOHSAPHOL SITIWATJANA
DONNIE YEN	JEAN CLAUDE VAN DAMME
FUNAKOSHI AWARD	*FUNAKOSHI AWARD*
DUKE TIRSCHEL	RAYMOND CHOW

CONTENTS

Events that Changed America, 23

2011 Hall of Fame Inductees

MIKE CHAT, 35
ADRIANO EMPERADO, 41
KEE HWANG, 47
JI HAN JAE, 53
TOM LAUGHLIN, 59
AL NOVAK, 65
DAN SEVERN, 71
LEUNG SHUM, 77
IN HYUK SUH, 83
CARL TOTTON, 89
KAREN MATSUDA, 95

2012 Hall of Fame Inductees

JUN CHONG, 99
KEIKO FUKUDA, 105
KAYLA HARRISON, 111
TAEJOON LEE, 117
TSUTOMU OHSHIMA, 123
KEN SHAMROCK, 129
ALEXANDER FU SHENG, 135
NAI KHANOM TOM, 141
ROGER TUNG, 147
KAM YUEN, 153
MICHAEL MATSUDA, 159

2013 Hall of Fame Inductees

LAU BUN, 167
PETER CUNNINGHAM, 173
ALAN GOLDBERG, 179
JAMES HONG, 185
MAKU IWAMATSU, 191
DAVE JOHNSON, 197
RICHARD RABAGO, 203
FELIX ROILES, 209
MARK SHUEY, 215
TINO TUIOLOSEGA, 221
ANNA MAY WONG, 227

2014 Hall of Fame Inductees

DAVID CARRADINE, 235
SAU CHUNG CHAN, 241
JOHN LEM, 247
ALBERT LEONG, 253
CHARLES LEWIS, 259
CHUCK LIDDELL, 265
JEFF SMITH, 271
CHUCK SULLIVAN, 277
CHEN KAUN TAI, 283
JAMES WING WOO, 289
OSAMU TEZUKA, 295

The Martial Arts History Museum's HALL OF FAME

Officially Recognizing those Key Individuals

Who Paved the Way for Us All

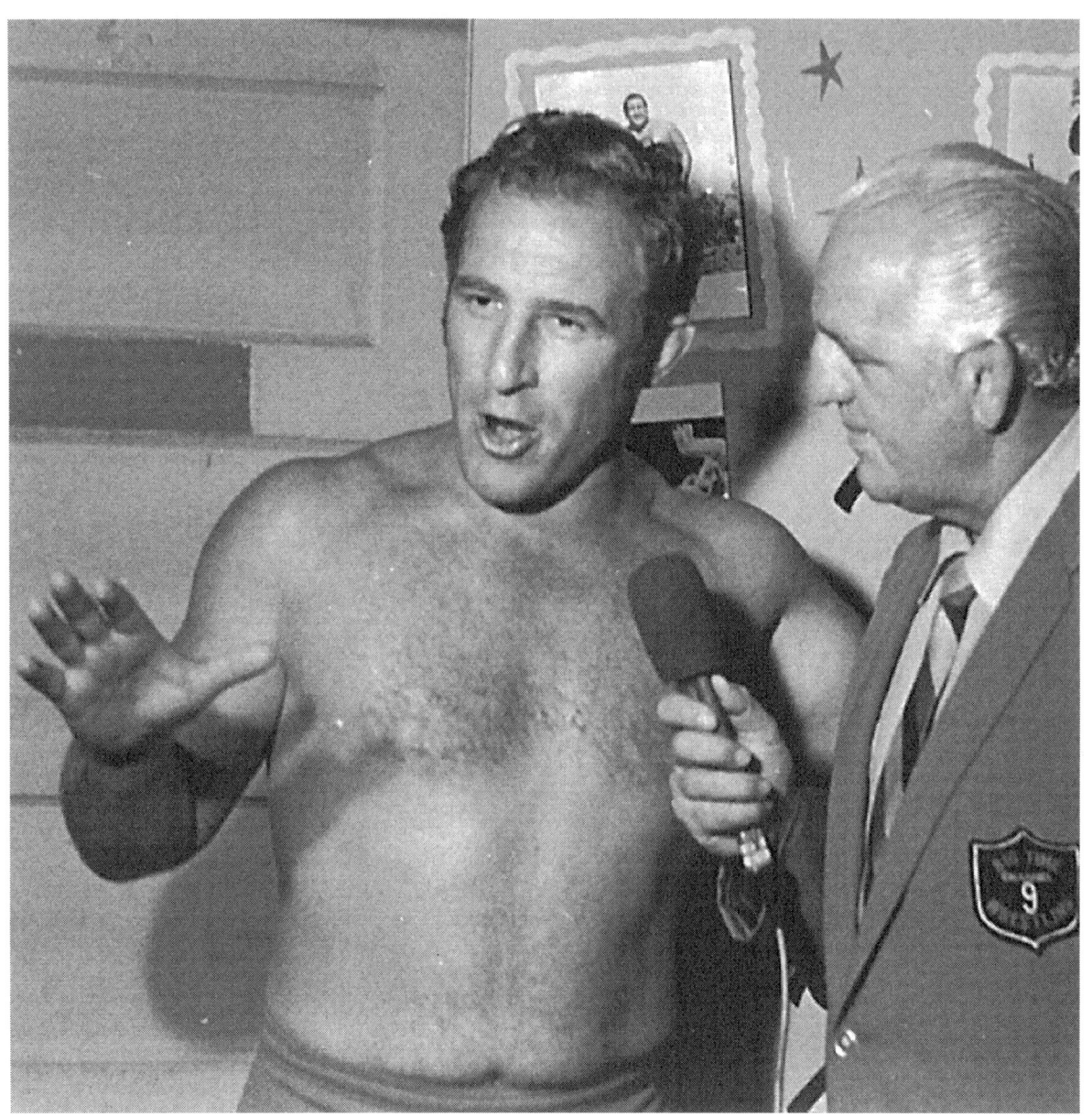

"JUDO" GENE LEBELL (2000) INTRODUCED THE ART OF JUDO INTO PROFESSIONAL WRESTLING.

THE MILESTONES IN MARTIAL ARTS HISTORY
Events that Changed America

There are many different ways to look at martial arts history in America. If you are as old as dirt as I am, you were there to experience it. I was just a little kid when the "blood and guts" era began, and tournaments started popping up all over the place. I remember Chuck Norris when he was just a competitor battling his arch-rival Joe Lewis. Gene LeBell was a Judo player that I was able to see at the Gardens.

KIM KAHANA (2018)

If you were lucky enough to live back then, you witnessed the famous Jim Harrison sweeps, the introduction of hand and foot pads, the breaking power of Jhoon Rhee, the nail hammering of Tak Kubota, and watching Kim Kahana, the most incredible martial arts stuntman ever!

If you were part of that generation, you might have witnessed a young

Karate student named Mike Dillard, who started a supply empire from his garage called Century Martial Arts, and Joe Jennings become the guru of video instruction. And, if you were older than that, you may have met the great Ark Y. Wong as he opened the doors of Kung Fu to the non-Chinese.

For martial arts history, it usually spread from Asia to Hawaii and from Hawaii to California, then across the nation and the world.

As the years passed, let's take a moment to look back and appreciate how the martial arts changed our lives for the better and how so many events had an impact on each of us.

KEITH VITALI (2019) AND MICHAEL DILLARD (2008).

The Milestones of Martial Arts History

People start taking martial arts for many different reasons. Many of us took martial arts because we were picked on in school. Others joined a school because their friends were doing it, while others were ordered by their parents to begin studying the arts. We all have our own personal history.

Through this article, I've taken a different approach to martial arts history. Instead of focusing on individuals, I wanted to take a brief look at specific events that changed the direction of the martial arts forever. These are events that made such a huge impact, that it can still be felt today.

So, if you will allow me, I have categorized these events into three milestones.

The First Milestone

Although the martial arts can be traced back thousands upon thousands of years, primarily in Asia, it wasn't until the 1800s that martial arts made its way to America and gained notoriety. It was around 1848 when gold was discovered in Northern California. At the time, China was going through a famine, and many Chinese immigrated to America in hopes of finding gold and then returning back home.

Unfortunately, little gold was ever found, and most Chinese remained in America working on the railroad. I do not doubt that some of them knew Kung Fu and probably taught others within their community.

It wouldn't be until nearly a hundred years later that the martial arts would finally gain national attention in the United States. In the 1940s, America was in the middle of a war with Japan. Hollywood began producing hundreds of war movies to support the war effort, but also took advantage of the situation. One of these movies made such an impact that it changed the martial arts world forever.

It was 1945, and the film "Blood on the Sun" was released in American theaters. Now, martial arts have always been in the movies going back as far as the silent films; one can see a glimpse of martial arts fighting. What made this film different, was that the most famous actor in the world, James Cagney, would have a scene fighting a Japanese opponent using martial arts.

Learning the art of Judo and Jiu-Jitsu to prepare himself, Cagney was able to showcase his newly discovered skill to defeat this opponent.

It was the first time a Caucasian star performed a Japanese form of martial arts in a film. As a result, everyone wanted to learn Judo, and just like that, Judo schools were popping up nationwide. From 1945 to 1964, Judo became the most popular martial art in America, so popular that it even became an Olympic Sport.

The Second Milestone

After World War II ended with Japan, U.S. military bases were established in Japan and Okinawa. Then, after the Korean war ended, bases were also erected in South Korea. Japanese and Korean teachers were hired to teach the military personnel to keep the troops in shape and learn different combative skills.

The classes were continually packed as

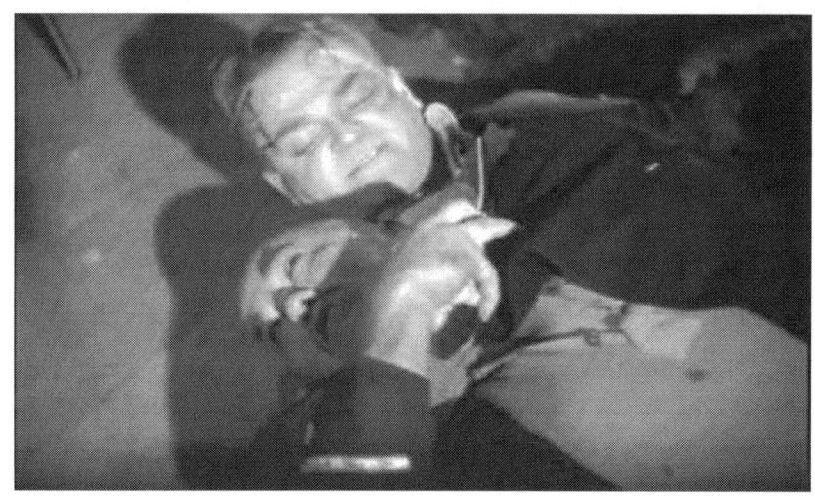
ACTOR JAMES CAGNEY USING JIU-JITSU IN THE FILM "BLOOD ON THE SUN".

American servicemen were introduced to various forms of martial arts. While stationed for two to four years, many became very accomplished in such arts as Karate and Tae Kwon Do.

After their tour of duty ended, soldiers returned home with some even opening a martial arts school. As early as 1946, the first commercial school run by a non-Asian, was established in Phoenix, Arizona.

Around the mid-1960s, a young Chuck Norris was stationed in Korea and began learning the art of Tang Soo Do. By then, Karate tournaments were in full swing, and when he returned to the states, Norris quickly became one of the top point fighters in the country.

In 1966, Chinese martial arts was finally introduced to America through a television series called "The Green Hornet" starring Bruce Lee.

But despite all this attention, martial arts was still relatively unknown.

TOM LAUGHLIN (2011) IN THE FILM, "BILLY JACK."

That was of course, until 1971, and the second and most significant milestone would appear in a film called "Billy Jack."

SHAW BROS. KUNG FU ACTOR TI LUNG (2017).

An actor/director/writer, Tom Laughlin wrote a film that would bring attention to the poor treatment that Native Americans were experiencing in America. In the movie, Laughlin would play a former Green Beret who became an expert in the art of Hapkido while stationed in Korea.

"Billy Jack" was the first time that the martial arts was a primary feature in a film. It became a box office hit!

Because of the success of that film, the Hong Kong movie producers, who had been producing Kung Fu movies for several years, saw a blossoming market and began shipping every martial arts movie they could create to American theaters. Companies such as the Shaw Bros. and Golden Harvest became household names as Kung Fu movies flooded the West.

It didn't take long before martial arts instructors began to open martial arts studios all over the country. From Kung Fu schools to Karate schools, American audiences couldn't get enough of the martial arts. Called by many as the "Kung Fu movie boom" or the "martial arts movie boom," everything changed, and martial arts was now part of everyone's lives.

Of all those films, the biggest star was Bruce Lee, and as a result, the world wanted to be just like him.

The Third Milestone

The year was 1984, and martial arts movies were at an all-time high. The Kung Fu movie boom continued and launched a series of American-made action films. Chuck Norris leaped from the tournament circuit into movie-making and became an instant sensation. Independent films featuring Don Wilson and Cynthia Rothrock dominated Blockbuster Video store shelves, and the Ninja craze was in full swing.

One day, a different kind of martial arts movie was about to be released, becoming the third milestone in martial arts history. Until then, most films were about shooting up the bad guys and using martial arts to crush the enemy; everything was geared toward an adult audience.

When the film "The Karate Kid" was released, it had a whole new approach. Instead of focusing on blowing up bad guys, it was about teenagers who were dealing with issues in growing up in high school. It featured an old, traditional Japanese Karate teacher who took a young Caucasian boy under his wing to prevent him from being bullied by a gang of black belts who had no respect for tradition.

ART CAMACHO (2003) AND CYNTHIA ROTHROCK (1999) ON THE SET OF "THE CAMACHO EXPERIEMENT" SHOW.

Starring Pat Morita and Ralph Macchio, it was the story of a teenager in his quest to confront his enemies at the local Karate tournament. The movie was so impressive it not only became the top film at the box office, but it introduced young people to the world of martial arts and Karate tournaments.

The Karate Kid film significantly affected the younger generation as thousands of kids began to enroll in martial arts schools. Because of the Karate Kid movie, Hollywood launched a series of kid-oriented martial arts films and television shows.

RALPH MACCHIO AND PAT MORITA (2015) IN "THE KARATE KID."

In time, Billy Blank's Tae bo and the Ultimate Fighting Championship (UFC) would significantly affect the martial arts community. Still, none could match the impact that occurred as a result of the three milestones.

As the great John Corcoran said, "Michael, we were there to see it happen."

I hope you enjoy volume four of the Martial Arts History Museum's Hall of Fame series.

The Hall of Fame Inductees

2011

Mike Chat	Al Novak
Adriano Emperado	Dan Severn
Kee Hwang	Leung Shum
Ji Han Jae	In Hyuk Suh
Tom Laughlin	Carl Totton

FUNAKOSHI AWARD WINNER
Karen Matsuda

The Evolution of the Revolution
Mike Chat

Mike Chaturantabut

BORN
April 30, 1975

BIRTHPLACE
Rayong Province, THAILAND

PRIMARY STYLE
Wu Shu, Tae Kwon Do

Michael Chaturantabut, or as he likes to be called, Michael Chat, became one of the most dynamic forces during the 1990s. Through his innovative and explosive kicking techniques to his unremarkable air-defying martial arts movements, Chat ushered in a new era for not only tournament competition, but added a new element for action fight choreography.

Looking back, the 1960s and 1970s tournament circuit was primarily dominated by traditional Asian martial arts styles. It wasn't until the 1980s that ultra-high kicking from the Korean artforms brought a new flare to the forms division of tournament competition.

Turning the clock forward to the 1990s, a new performance concept would revolutionize sport Karate and the

entire martial arts community. Called Xtreme Martial Arts, better known as XMA, it set a new standard in martial arts tournament competitions. The brainchild of martial artist, actor, and stuntman Mike Chat, XMA is a combination of martial arts, acrobatic elements, and gymnastics, emphasizing performance showmanship.

Like the sport of "tricking," which combines gymnastics and tumbling, XMA takes it a step further by employing open-handed choreography with dramatic dance, high-flying acrobatic maneuvers, and martial arts striking and kicking.

Chat believes that using the martial arts as its foundation; it can be expanded to be more flashy and artistic.

Starting with the tournament circuit's showmanship division and moving into forms and weapons, XMA gave the impression of complexity and difficulty as they wowed the crowds and judges.

Through the partnership of Chat and his wife, McKenzie Satterthwaite, they designed and launched their first XMA martial arts performance training program. To date, XMA has developed into a complete teaching system with over 1,300 schools licensed to teach the XMA curriculum.

Chat uses a combination of several traditional martial arts styles, including Okinawan Shorei-ryu, Tae Kwon Do, Chinese Kung Fu, Wu Shu, and Kickboxing.

It wasn't long before Hollywood noticed Chat as he landed several nationally televised commercials highlighting his skills.

His success in Hollywood continued as he landed a starring role in Fox's #1 hit TV show, "WMAC Masters," where he debuted his own character creation, the Wizard.

Chat's string of luck took him onto the set of the ever-popular "Mighty Morphin Power Rangers Light Speed Rescue" series as Chad Lee, the Blue Power Ranger.

Mike Chat combined the old style elements with the flamboyant style of the new and raised competition to a new level.

One of the Five Founders of Kajukenbo
Adriano Emperado

Adriano Directo Emperado

BORN
June 15, 1926

DIED
April 5, 2009

BIRTHPLACE
Honululu,
Hawaii
USA

PRIMARY STYLE
Kajukenbo

Adriano Emperado is credited as one of the primary founders and the most prominent advocate of a uniquely developed artform called Kajukenbo. A new system developed by five martial arts experts who felt that by selecting the most effective movements and techniques from their own system, they would be able to form a more practical way of fighting.

These individuals included Peter Choo, a welterweight boxing champion and a black belt in Tang Soo Do; Frank Ordonez, an expert in Sekeino Jiu-

ADRIANO EMPERADO (2011) WITH CARRIE OGAWA-WONG (2005) AND DOUGLAS WONG (2002).

Jitsu; Joe Holke, 8th degree black belt in Kodokan Judo; Clarence Chang, an expert in Siu Lum P'ai Kung Fu and Emperado, a 5th degree black belt in Kara-Ho Kenpo. The name Kajukenbo is a combination of the various arts from which its style is derived: KA for Karate, JU for Judo and Jujutsu, KEN for Kenpo and BO for Boxing.

It was around 1945 when the group got together to formulate this new system. Unfortunately, America was still involved in a war and the other four founders were drafted into the military. This left the development of Kajukenbo in the hands of Emperado.

It took him several years to refine the system but in 1950, Adriano Emperado opened the first Kajukenbo school in Palama, Hawaii, his hometown, at the Palama Settlement Gym. Although he had extensive training in martial arts throughout his life, he was more practitioner than an instructor. Explaining to his students, "You have to experience pain before you can give it. The workout wasn't over until there was blood on the floor."

The students quickly understood his meaning after the first class, and as Emperado put it, "we lost a lot of students in those days." However, according to him, they got new students, including black belts from other schools, because of his no-nonsense practical teachings."

It wasn't long until Emperado started extending his teaching to several classes. He opened an additional school at the Kaimuki YMCA and another course at the Wahiawa YMCA.

Upon the return of his companions, they continued to contribute and perfect the art. As a result, together they launched a series of schools throughout Hawaii and became the longest chain of Karate schools worldwide.

It was these five men who examined the weaknesses of their style and found better methods of application. Before mixed martial arts was even a term, these individuals were already promoting the best methods from their backgrounds.

Emperado was born to Filipino Hawaiian parents in the poverty-stricken section of Honolulu in the Palama district. It was a violent place to live; confrontations and fights were daily.

He started self-defense training as a necessity. At the age of eight, his father and uncle, who were professional boxers, trained him how defend himself.

At 14, he began his training in Judo; however, he didn't start training seriously until he was 20 years old. This was at the Catholic youth organization in Honolulu in the art of Kenpo under the legendary William K.S. Chow.

Emperado became the first black belt awarded by Chow. In time, he eventually earned his 5th degree. He served as a harbor police officer for the Hawaii dept. of transportation and later as a bodyguard to the governor.

He also became immersed in studying the art of Escrima with his stepfather, Alfredo Peralta. He also studied Choy Li Fut with icon Lau Bun and Northern style Shaolin with Sifu Wong.

Although each man receives the credit for their contribution to Kajukenbo, Emperado is the one who built the foundation of the art and began its promotion throughout the islands.

Creating Tang Soo Do Moo Kuk Kwan
Hwang Kee

Hwang Kee

BORN
November 9, 1914

DIED
July 14, 2002

BIRTHPLACE
Jang Dan,
Kyong Ki Province
SOUTH KOREA

PRIMARY STYLE
Tang Soo Do

In 1921, when Hwang Kee was only seven years old, he had his first experience in the martial arts. It was at a nearby festival that he and his family attended. The sights and sounds were astounding, with many unforgettable exhibits, including an archery and a wrestling demonstration.

While his family enjoyed their time at the event, a dispute broke out nearby. There was one man being surrounded by a group of seven or eight men. Suddenly, the gang attacked the lone man. Amazingly, the man evaded their every strike and countered back,

attacking them with punches and especially kicks. It wasn't long until the lone man defeated every member of the group. As a result, Kee was so impressed with the man's skill that he followed him home that evening. In time, he went to the man's house and asked if he could become his student. Sadly, the man's refused to teach him because he felt he was too young to learn the art.

For Hwang Kee, that was unacceptable. It was important that he learn this man's fighting style. Fortunately for him, there was a hill overlooking the man's house, and he could see straight into his backyard. The man practiced an artform called Tae Kyun, and he would teach a group of students at the back of his house every afternoon. So, Hwang Kee decided to sneak out as much as possible and watch the man's class from the hilltop.

Hwang Kee would spend hours watching them and imitating their movements. Although this was not his formal introduction to the martial arts,

Kee took it seriously as he practiced every technique he saw. He continued his "far away" instruction for several years.

Born in 1914, Korea was occupied by the Japanese military. His father was a scholar and teacher who insisted that his son finish high school despite the Japanese military being present. At the time, most students never completed their schooling.

Upon graduating, Hwang Kee took a job working for the Manchurian Railroad in China. It was there that he began his formal training in the martial arts. There, he was taught a Korean artform called Kuk Sool under a Chinese teacher named Yank Kunk Jin. It was also during this time, that Kee was introduced to a style of martial arts called the Tang style.

In 1937, Hwang Kee returned to Korea to continue his martial arts education. Unfortunately, studying any form of martial arts was very limited because the Japanese was still in Korea. Therefore, to keep his martial skills sharp, he went to the local library to check out Okinawan Karate books. So impressed by what he was reading, Kee would check out every book on Shotokan Karate.

Over the next several years, Hwang Kee successfully incorporated the teachings and philosophies of Shotokan into the traditional Korean martial arts methodology. He first called his newfound system, "Hwa Soo Do Moo Kuk Kwan," and opened his first school in 1945. Kee became one of the first group of teachers to openly teach a Korean art form as soon as the occupation ended. Sadly, his first two attempts at running a school were unsuccessful.

By 1950, with the occupation entirely ended and he decided to change the system's name to Tang Soo Do Moo Kuk Kwan.

In 1957, Kee noted that he discovered a woodblock print illustrating indigenous Korean martial arts. It dated back to 1790, and Kee studied the book and incorporated many of these moves into his system.

From 1953 to 1960, Tang Soo Do Moo Do Kuk became one of the most prominent organizations in Korea, with nearly 75% of all martial artists studying his form of fighting.

Hwang Kee stepped into history by blending the traditional techniques of the Korean art forms with the movements of Shotokan to form Tang Soo Do. Today, such figures as Chuck Norris have popularized the art.

The Pioneer of Hapkido
Ji Han-Jae

Ji Han Jae

BORN
August 14, 1936

BIRTHPLACE
Andong,
Gyeongsangbuk-do,
SOUTH KOREA

PRIMARY STYLE
Hapkido

Ji Han-Jae is considered as one of the highest-ranking instructors in the Korean art of Hapkido, a 10th-degree black belt. Many have even said that he coined the term, "Hapkido."

Ji was born on August 17, 1936, in Andong, South Korea. To provide better living conditions for their son and to flee the Japanese occupation, his family moved to Sun Yang, China, when he was just a one-year-old. Ji Han Jae attended school there until he was nine years old, which was around 1945. It was then that the war ended, and so many Korean families were returning back to Korea.

Around 1953, several years after their return to Korea, Ji Han-Jae took his first step into the martial arts world. The artform he began studying was called Yawara (which would later be referred to as Hapkido) with teacher Choi Yong Sul. Although Choi didn't have a commercial school, he had been teaching for years out of his home in Taegu City.

Choi's training introduced Ji Han-Jae to several unique martial arts movements, including joint locks, grappling techniques, and throws.

Three years later, when Ji Han-Jae was 20, he moved back to his hometown of Andong. It was there that Ji opened his first martial arts school that he called, An Mu Kwan.

The father of one of his students was a respected martial arts teacher named Taoist Lee. Lee introduced Ji to a unique set of weapons training which included the staff and the short stick.

Lee also taught him the art of Taek-Kyun, which included a variety of high jumping and kicking techniques. Ji felt the additional kicking techniques

would be an excellent complement to the lessons taught to him by Choi Yong Sul.

Ji Han-Jae continued to learn different aspects of the arts, including numerous meditation and breathing exercises.

In 1958, Ji Han-Jae moved his school to Joong Boo Shi Jang, where he decided to combine the meditation techniques with the jump kicking movements that he had learned. For a while, he was joined by his former classmate from Choi's school, Sung Moo Kwan.

Ji Han-Jae also decided to rename the school calling it "Hapki-Yoo-

Kwan-Sool." Feeling that the name was too long, he changed it to "Hapkido."

In 1961, Ji began teaching Hapkido at the military academy and later received a government position teaching the art of the president's security forces.

In 1969, Ji Han-Jae came to America as part of an exchange with President Nixon's security forces. There, he taught Hapkido to the secret service, special forces, FBI and CIA. At the same time, he was visiting Andrews Air Force Base, where a friend of his, Tae Kwon Do legend Jhoon Rhee, introduced him to Bruce Lee.

Since Bruce was absorbing every martial arts style like a sponge, he asked Ji Han-Jae to show him some movements. So impressed with his techniques, he asked Ji to appear as one of his evil opponents in a film he was working on called "The Game of Death."

Building upon the foundation of Choi Yong Sool, incorporating the unique kicking methods of Tae-Kyun, and enhancing the arts with proper meditation, Ji Han-Jae became one of Hapkido's greatest pioneers.

The Man Who Started It All
Tom Laughlin

Tom Laughlin

BORN
August 10, 1931

DIED
December 12, 2013

BIRTHPLACE
Milwaukee,
Wisconsin
USA

PRIMARY STYLE
Hapkido

In 1972, an American independent film made its way into theatrical release and forever changed the martial arts world.

That film was "Billy Jack." Starring a fresh young actor named Tom Laughlin, who decided to write a screenplay about the poor treatment of Native Americans in the United States. The movie not only opened the doors to Western audiences about Native American traditions but also introduced a new cultural element, the Eastern method of combat.

The main character, Billy Jack, is a former green beret whose military training included Asian forms of martial arts.

In this particular case, it was the Korean art of Hapkido. This would be the first time that the martial arts is featured as a primary part of the film.

The movie became a blockbuster hit in America. The Shaw Brothers, a Hong Kong film production company, also noticed. The Shaw Brothers had been producing Kung Fu period-themed films for some time. It wasn't until the success of Billy Jack that they believed that American audiences were now ready for their style of martial arts revenge movies, and they were right.

As a result, Hong Kong-made films were being rapidly shipped to America. In movies like "The Five Fingers of Death" to the "Flying Guillotine," American audiences couldn't get enough of martial arts films.

Billy Jack lit the fire and started the biggest martial arts movie boom in history. At first, it was just Kung Fu films, but other types of Asian martial arts films began to appear.

As a result, martial arts schools were emerging out of nowhere. From Kung Fu schools to Karate schools to Tae Kwon Do schools, martial arts schools were opening in YMCA's, community centers, and storefronts.

Tom Laughlin did not start as a martial artist, but after witnessing a demonstration from Hapkido pioneer Bong Soo Han, he was so impressed that he wanted to make the martial arts a crucial part of the film.

In Billy Jack, the star takes on a town full of bad guys headed by a corrupt sheriff. To defend himself and the inhabitants of a small Native American

village, he uses his martial arts skills which were more than impressive.

His teacher, Hapikdo legend Bong Soo Han, actually did all the incredible kicking scenes.

Billy Jack was a sequel to the movie "Born Losers" in which his character was introduced. After the success of Billy Jack, his second film, "The Trial of Billy Jack" also became a blockbuster hit. In this film, he included his instructor

as a principal character.

Billy Jack was released in 1973, and Tom Laughlin and Bong Soo Han traveled all over America, giving martial arts demonstrations.

Over the years, Laughlin took a strong political stand campaigning for term limits, tax cuts, public education, and nuclear disarmament. He even ran for the office of the president of the United States as a Democratic and Republican candidate.

Although Laughlin had limited martial arts training, his film, Billy Jack, became the Olympic torch that set the world on fire.

INSIDE KUNG-FU

OUTSIDE U.S.A. $1.25 $1.00
THE ULTIMATE IN MARTIAL ARTS COVERAGE!

VOL. 4, NO. 2 APRIL 1977

**Al Novak's Gung Fu
It's the Real Thing**

JEET KUNE DO

**Ark Wong Grand Master
of the 5 Animal System**

The White Lotus Style

**The Drunken Style
of Kung Fu**

The First Non-Chinese Kung Fu Artist/Teacher
Al Novak

Al Novak

BORN
1924

DIED
November 26, 2011

BIRTHPLACE
Milwaukee, Wisconsin
USA

PRIMARY STYLE
Kung Fu

At the same time gold was discovered in California, a famine swept across China in the mid-1800s. To feed their families, many Chinese immigrants packed up their belongings and headed to America in search of gold to make a better life for themselves. Since very little gold was found, many Chinese worked on the railroad; but with them, they brought their art, food, way of life, and of course, Kung Fu.

Unlike the Japanese community, who openly taught their forms of martial arts to anyone willing to learn, the Chinatowns of the day restricted their teachings to the tongs and specific Chinese groups. It was forbidden to teach the Caucasians, which they called the "gwailo." It would be nearly a hundred years before Kung Fu was taught openly.

Since then, many people have claimed that they were the first non-Chinese to learn Kung Fu. Because Ark Y. Wong was considered the first instructor to teach non-Chinese commercially in 1959, they would likely be rooted back to him.

However, one individual actually dates back even further than the 1950s: it was Al Novak.

Novak is considered the earliest practitioner and the first non-Chinese student and teacher of Chinese Kung Fu. Recognized and highly respected by the community, he was invited to every major event. His friends and students chauffeured him, and every promoter happily gave him a ring-side seat and an all-access pass.

Back in the 1930s, martial arts instruction was practically non-existent in America. In fact, most people had never even heard of Karate, Kung Fu or even Judo for that matter.

Realizing that finding a class to learn martial arts was practically impossible, so in 1939, Novak began his study in the martial arts through a mail-order correspondence course he found in the back of a magazine. It was

one of those gadget magazines.

The style advertised in the magazine was Kano Jiu-Jitsu which he faithfully practiced every day for several years until he finally located the actual school where the book came from in Milwaukee, Wisconsin. He relocated there and studied with the class for a year and a half.

When World War II broke out, Novak was stationed in Hawaii, where he continued practicing the Jiu-Jitsu movements he learned in class. It wouldn't be long until he was introduced to Kajukenbo, a combination of Chinese and other Asian artforms. The course was taught by Adriano Emperado.

Upon his discharge from the military, Novak settled in the San Francisco

Bay area. At the time, there was a massive influx of Chinese immigrants to the area. This proved to be a golden opportunity to Novak. He befriended many of the immigrants and one of them happened to be a Si Lum Fat Gar Kung Fu teacher named T.Y. Wong. Immediately they hit it off as Novak helped him adjust to Western society. To repay his kindness, Wong started teaching Novak privately in his basement and it was there, in the mid-1940s, that Novak stepped into history as the first non-Chinese to study Kung Fu.

In 1958, Novak met teacher Jimmy Lee who was a brick-breaking expert. Novak saw Lee doing a palm brick-breaking demonstration at one of Wally Jay's luaus. Jay would throw these lavish luaus every year, and the who's who of the martial arts would attend. Novak was so impressed that he also began to train under Jimmy Lee. In time, Novak would be considered the face of iron palm breaking in America. He would be featured in many magazines, including Ring magazine and Popular Science magazine.

At Jimmy Lee's place, Novak met a young Bruce Lee. Together they

talked about the idea of Bruce Lee opening up a commercial school. It wasn't long until Bruce Lee eventually decided to open a Jun Fan Gung Fu school.

Novak was unlike any other individual. Even though the Chinese Kung Fu instructors were traditionally not allowed to teach non-Chinese, for some reason, he was welcomed by the community with open arms.

According to Novak, he never felt discriminated against, and every teacher he met was more than happy to have him under their wing.

The Beast of the UFC
Dan Severn

Dan Severn

BORN
June 8, 1958

BIRTHPLACE
Coldwater,
Michigan
USA

PRIMARY STYLE
Wrestling, Judo

The martial arts have continued to evolve in many different directions. From traditional to acrobatic, from point fighting to full-contact Karate to Kickboxing. Today, mixed martial arts have become the newest evolution. Using a combination of wrestling maneuvers, Jiu-Jitsu grappling and a little street brawling, mixed martial arts gained widespread recognition in 1993, primarily through an organization called the United Fighting Championships (UFC). One of those early competitors who stepped into the ring and helped pioneer the art was Dan "the Beast" Severn.

A UFC Triple Crown Champion, Severn is considered one of the world's most successful mixed martial artists. He was the winner of both the UFC Superfight Championship and the 1995 Ultimate Tournament. He has competed in nearly every mixed martial arts league including King of the Cage, Pride FC, Cage Rage, WEC, RINGS and MFC and set a professional record of 101-19-7.

Severn was also a professional wrestler as a two-time NWA World

Heavyweight Champion reigning for over four years. He was the first to compete in the UFC and the World Wrestling Federation simultaneously. Severn is one of the greatest world record holders winning 13 championships belts.

Born and raised in Coldwater, Michigan, he grew up on a farm tending to the animals and getting his hands dirty. Sports extremely influenced Severn at a very young age. In Jr. High School, he was part of the basketball team. It was also then, in his teens, that he started learning Jiu-Jitsu, wrestling and Greco-Roman wrestling.

When he reached high school, he wanted to be part of the high school wrestling team.

It was then that Severn caught a lucky break when his high school

wrestling coach asked him to be a fill-in for the amateur wrestling team. For some reason, most of the team had gotten sick, so they had a shortage and needed Severn to fill in on the team. His performance was so impressive that

he was never asked to fill-in ever again and the coach placed him on the team. In fact, he was named the most "Outstanding High School Wrestler in the Nation," and this was before his 18th birthday.

He later became a two-time All-American at the Arizona State University and became a U.S. Olympic Team alternate. For the 1984 Olympic trials, he lost the final qualifying match to eventual gold medal winner Lou Banach. Severn says it was a match that he credits helped inspire him.

After completing his bachelor's degree program at the university, he

 began entering many wrestling events. From 1982 to 1994, he traveled all over the world competing. The events took him to Japan, Hungary, Cuba, France, and Turkey. It was also during this time that Severn started competing in Judo events.

Severn also tried his hand at coaching wrestling at ASU and Michigan State University.

It was in 1993 that the United Fighting Championships began. It was an unknown factor with no clear direction, but it played the most significant role in bringing worldwide attention to mixed martial arts. One year after its inception, Dan Severn stepped into history by competing in the fourth event called the UFC 4 Championships. He was pitted against one of the event's creator's family members, Royce Gracie. This was a new field of fighting that would change the world, and Severn became a part of it as one of its earliest pioneers.

Dan Severn returned in UFC 5 with a vengeance defeating Russian Oleg Taktaroy.

Over the years, Severn continued to dominate in competition as he eventually became a role model for mixed martial arts and an icon for taking a chance on a brand sport that became a new norm for the martial arts industry.

Bringing Eagle Claw Kung Fu to America
Leung Shum

Leung Shum

BORN
April 30, 1952

BIRTHPLACE
Hong Kong,
CHINA

PRIMARY STYLE
Eagle Claw Kung Fu

Leung Shum began his training at an early age, when he was only eight years old. The style was Eagle Claw Kung Fu. This took place in Kowloon, Hong Kong. The teacher was sifu Ng Wai Nung who happened to be his godfather. Although the school was quite small, 30 students packed the place. According to Shum, with so many students crammed into one school, this made it very challenging to learn.

Although jammed with students, Leung Shum was so impressed with Eagle Claw, that he never chose to learn any other style for the rest of his life.

The class, however, didn't seem to have any structure.

First, the students warmed up by stretching on their own. After which, they did their own exercises, and then the Sifu would come in and start teaching them forms, weaponry, and techniques.

It was also during this time, that there was a lot of turmoil in the nation, and the government made sparring illegal. Since they couldn't fight in the class, they tested their skills in the streets.

After many years of studying with his godfather, Sifu Ng received a letter from a friend in Singapore asking him to come to Singapore for three years to help him set up a school. He accepted the invitation and put Leung Shum with his Kung Fu brothers in charge of the Kowloon school until their teacher returned.

Three years had gone by and Sifu Ng returned to the school, but saw that only Leung Shum remained teaching. Shum would continue at the school for 16 years as his assistant instructor. In 1971, Shum decided to move to the United States.

Unfortunately, coming to America to open an Eagle Claw school would be more difficult than he could have anticipated. It was one year before the big "Kung Fu movie boom," so no one had even heard the term, Kung Fu, let alone Eagle Claw Kung Fu. To pay the bills, he worked as a dishwasher at a local Chinese restaurant.

For the next year, he walked the streets greeting people and trying to make friends within the Chinese community. By doing a few small demonstrations here and there, he met the instructor of the Tiger style class,

sifu Wai Hong. Sifu Hong organized a martial arts tournament and invited Leung Shum to be one of the judges and to give a demonstration as well.

Even within the tournament circuit, Eagle Claw was non-existent; that is until Leung Shum performed the art on stage.

One particular audience member, a Caucasian individual, named Don Larkin was so impressed by his moves, that he sought him out after the event and asked him to be his teacher.

Don Larkin became his first student in America. Since Leung Shum didn't have a school, Larkin took private lessons at his home. In 1974, Larkin helped his teacher by assisting him in opening the first Eagle Claw Kung Fu school in America in New York City.

Leung Shum admitted that teaching Kung Fu in the West differed greatly from the training he underwent. When he was young, the teacher would devote a whole year to learning just one form, inside and out. But in the West, his teachings had to be adjusted to a class structure with students progressing from technique to technique at an accelerated pace.

Nevertheless, Leung Shum was able to strike a balance in his teachings. The training was very strict. Students weren't able to progress to the next movement until they met his satisfaction. Because of this, his students were amazing.

Over the next several decades, Leung Shum was able to enlighten thousands of students in the art of Eagle Claw. Many of his advanced students have been with him for over 30 years.

Leung Shum took on the role of not only the first to bring Eagle Claw to America, but he became its most prominent advocate by promoting the art across the world.

The Pioneer of Kuk Sool Won
In Hyuk Suh

In Hyuk Su

BORN
December 21, 1960

BIRTHPLACE
Elizabeth,
New Jersey
USA

PRIMARY STYLE
Kuk Sool Won

The year was 1910, and everything changed for Korea. Japan had begun its occupation of the Korean peninsula enforcing strict military guidelines, including their ban on Korean martial arts. Fortunately for In Hyuk Suh, he started his martial arts training before the occupation. He was only five when his grandfather Myung-Duk Suh hand-picked him to be his student. Myung-Duk Suh was a much herald teacher of Korean martial arts. In fact, he served as a master instructor in the Korean Royal Courts.

As Japanese soldiers spread further across Korea, Myung-Duk Suh continued training his grandson in hiding. By the time In Hyuk Suh had reached 12 years old, he had already been studying for seven years.

Sadly, his grandfather was killed by Japanese troops. However, to prepare for an uncertainty like this, his grandfather made sure that his grandson would have the opportunity to continue his training by preparing a special letter

of introduction that would ensure acceptance by specific prominent Korean instructors.

The letter worked and for the next eight years, In Hyuk Suh began his journey throughout Korea, seeking the teachers to whom the letters were addressed. Always taught in places hidden from the military, In Hyuk Suh learned various Korean artforms from many different Korean teachers.

By 1945, the Japanese occupation had ended, and Korea began re-establishing its art, language, and martial arts.

Using his grandfather's teaching as his foundation, In Hyuk Suh began to compile all the teachings he learned. From the joint-locking techniques of Hapkido, the explosive kicking techniques of Tae Kwon Do, the falling moves found in Judo, the punching style of Tang Soo Do and the animal-style movements of Kung Fu, In Hyuk Suh took a step into history when he founded his own Korean system in 1958 that he called Kuk Sool Won.

The term Kuk Sool Won is broken into three parts: Kuk translates to Nation-State or Country. Sool means martial arts techniques that are of spiritual, cultural, and philosophical heritage of Korea, and Won, which means institution or association. In 1961, the Kuk Sool Won Association was officially established.

Taking another historical step, in 1974, In Hyuk Suh officially introduced Kuk Sool Won to the United States, thus moving its headquarters from Pusan, South Korea, to San Francisco, California. In 1991, the headquarters were relocated once more to Houston, Texas.

For the next six decades, the Kuk Sool Won organization now boasts 1.3 million members with over 800 schools worldwide in 27 different countries. In Hyuk Suh established the first Kuk Sool Won tournament in 1982 and continued to spread the art through books, instructional videos, demonstrations, and seminars. He has appeared in numerous martial arts magazines, gracing its covers several times.

In Hyuk Suh was able to carry on the traditions of his grandfather throughout Korea and across the world.

The Legend, the Kung Fu Icon, the Historian
Carl Totton

Carl Totton

BORN
March 9, 1948 ?

BIRTHPLACE
Los Angeles,
California
USA

PRIMARY STYLE
Kung Fu

Dr. Carl Totton is considered one of the most celebrated and iconic figures in martial arts history. Although known by many as a teacher of Northern style Shaolin Kung Fu, Dr. Totton has spent his entire life learning and training with some of the most significant figures in martial arts history.

A private student under the "Father of Kung Fu in America," Ark Y. Wong, to Kenpo legend Ed Parker to Chi

Kung sifu Share Lew to Lima Lama's Tiny Lefiti, Dr. Totton spent not just months but years training from over 60 teachers learning all aspects of the martial arts.

Although Dr. Totton became a widely respected teacher, he is, without a doubt, one of the world's greatest Chinese Kung Fu historians. A martial arts student since the mid-1960s, he can boast without hesitation: that he was there at nearly every major martial arts event, from being a judge at the early stages of the famous Long Beach International Karate Championships to the introduction of Wu Shu in America. He was a member of the first Kung Fu competition team in open Karate tournaments and was part of the launching of Inside Kung Fu magazine. He isn't just a holder of the archives, but a participant.

However, one of the unique things about Dr. Totton, and probably his greatest accomplishment, is his dedication to Chinese healing and the internal arts.

A protégé under Taoist meditation teacher Share Lew, Dr. Totton carried the torch of healing, mediation, and spiritual growth into the next generation and established the Taoist Institute. He is also certified as both a Reiki master and a Qigong expert.

Dr. Totton stepped into history by bringing to life the benefits of traditional Chinese internal and external artforms. Using the ancient Chinese methods of acupressure massage and medical Qigong, he has taught at five colleges and universities the uniqueness of traditional Oriental medicine.

Dr. Carl Totton was born and raised in Los Angeles and began his martial arts training in 1961 by a group of friends showing him Choy Li Fut Kung Fu and Goju-ryu Karate. In 1963, his formal instruction began with John Leoning, senior student Kajukenpo great Adriano Emperado. In 1966, he studied mind force principles of Aikido with sensei Isao Takahashi. Additional training came from sensei Koichi Tohei, and Southern Chinese Kung Fu, and White Eyebrow style with sifu Richard Wan.

In 1967, he and his close friends Doug Wong, Tom Chan, and Wilson Quan formed the Sil Lum Kung Fu Association and opened a school in Southern California. Together, they created the Sil Lum competition team and dominated the tournament circuit by winning over 500 trophies.

Dr. Totton studied with Ralph Shu and Samoan Haumea "Tiny" Lefiti before training privately with Ark Y. Wong. He also studied with Tino Tuiolosega and for 25 years with Share Lew.

He is not only a doctor of psychology from Pepperdine University, he is also a professor teaching classes on clinical psychology. He is a published author and a historian for the Martial Arts History Museum.

Dr. Totton believed, like his teacher Ark Y. Wong, "If you can hurt them, you can heal them."

Internal medicine, acupressure, and healing have also been essential to Chinese Kung Fu. But, through the years, only small fragments of the spiritual side of Kung Fu remain because of historical figures such as the great, Dr. Carl Totton.

"2011 Funakoshi Award Winner"

Changing the Future of the Museum

Karen Matsuda

If one had to identify a single individual who put the museum on the map, it would be Karen Matsuda. Wife of the museum's founder, Michael Matsuda, Karen took the reigns as the museum's Chief Financial Officer and within only a few months, not only registered the museum, but established its non-profit status in the first round (a feat that usually takes six months to do).

Although the museum was established in 1999, Michael took the museum on the road as a traveling exhibit. Borrowing every historical item he could find, he tested the market to see if it was worth pursuing a museum. A few years later, he was satisfied the community would support such an effort, and that's when Karen stepped in.

As CFO, she established the museum protocols, formalized the museum board, and handled the entire accounting process to keep the museum operational. Although Michael filled out the grant applications, Karen provided all the financial requests.

For the museum events, such as the dinner ceremonies, she handles all the tickets and works with the hotel to meet all their demands regarding insurance and food selections.

Karen also heads up the entire financial requirements for running Dragonfest. From determining the layout and managing the team for ticket sales to setting up and tearing down, Dragonfest would not run smoothly without her. In fact, the old Dragonfest used to have a line that was a quarter-mile long because it took several minutes to process ticket sales. Now, the line is at most ten people because she streamlined the process to just 30 seconds.

In addition to all the paperwork she must complete every week and the IRS forms she needs to submit constantly, she manages the funds to keep the museum alive and maintain our 501(c)(3) status. She also does double and triple duty working with Michael to clean the museum with janitorial duties.

Because of her support, the museum is not just a reality but has enabled it to exist independently. She has helped steer the museum in the right direction, and as a result, we were able to survive covid, even with a nearly 2-year lockdown.

Hats off to Karen for sticking with Michael, as they sacrificed so much financially to make this museum a reality and benefit the entire martial arts community.

The Hall of Fame Inductees

2012

Jun Chong	Ken Shamrock
Keiko Fukudo	Alexander Fu Sheng
Kayla Harrison	Nai Khanom Tom
Taejoon Lee	Roger Tung
Tsutomu Ohshima	Kam Yuen

FUNAKOSHI AWARD WINNER
Michael Matsuda

Tae Kwon Do Great
Jun Chong

Jun Chong

BORN
January 01, 1944

BIRTHPLACE
South Korea

PRIMARY STYLE
Tae Kwon Do

Jun Chong was born in South Korea in 1944. He was raised by a single mother who encouraged him to learn martial arts when he was just seven years old. His teacher's name was master Jho, and his style of martial art was Tae Kwon Do. Jun Chong was very shy at the time, so the art was difficult for him at first, but he immediately fell in love with the art.

Chong immersed himself in Tae Kwon Do and soon trained over eight hours daily. He continued his training for another seven years. When he reached junior high school, he wanted to test his skill by entering Karate tournaments. He enjoyed them so much that he kept entering contest after contest for another three years.

Jun Chong always dreamed of coming to America and opening his own Tae Kwon Do school.

During the 1960s, he also began training in the art of Hapkido under Sea Oh Choi, the founder of the art.

While studying with Sea Oh Choi, he studied other artforms, including Judo, Aikido, and Western-style boxing.

In the early 1970s, his dream of coming to America came true. He first began teaching for a Tae Kwon Do school in Los Angeles and then, in 1973, he decided to open up his own school in the city of Rosemead.

To promote the school, Chong performed countless demonstrations and performances. Trained by rigorous, perfectionist-style teachers, Chong's movements became extremely impressive.

1973 was a good year for the martial arts as "Enter the Dragon" and hundreds of Kung Fu movies began to flood the American market. As a result, martial arts schools were reaping the benefits as Chong was able to sign up 120 in just six months.

Over the next several years, Jun Chong met a variety of teachers, performers, and competitors. One, in particular, was a Tang Soo Do teacher named Chuck Norris. Norris was running a school on Wilshire Blvd. in Beverly Hills, which was an ideal location because many of Hollywood's elite stars lived there. Norris' film career was taking off, and he needed to sell the school.

In 1975, two years after opening his Rosemead school, Jun Chong leaped at the opportunity and purchased Chuck Norris' school. The Beverly Hills school became his headquarters as Chong opened several schools in Southern California.

Martial arts and action-style movies continued to grow, and highly skilled martial artists like Jun Chong were in high demand. He started as a stuntman and then worked his way to fight choreography. Soon he was playing principal roles, and within just a few short years, he formed his own production company.

Called Action Brothers Production, Inc., Jun Chong started producing several independent films, including "Ninja Turf," "Silent Assassins," "Street Soldiers," and "Johnny's Victory."

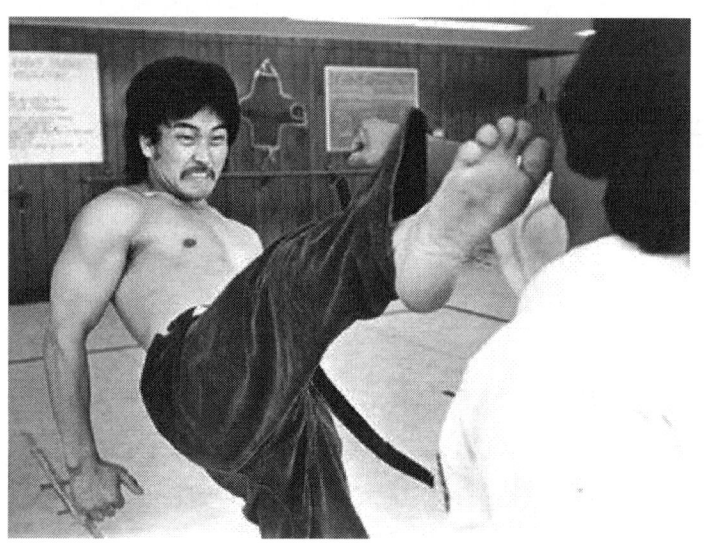

To promote Tae Kwon Do across the globe, he created the World United Martial Arts Organization, which would connect martial arts schools worldwide.

Chong continued to emphasize traditional training methods, which he would reinforce by hosting seminars, workshops, and a video instruction series and authored a number of published books.

Jun Chong's school became one of the most respected and successful schools in Southern California. He has taught thousands of students over the past four decades and helped establish Tae Kwon Do in the West. Many students have carried on the torch by promoting Tae Kwon Do through film and television productions. Some of those included are Phillip Rhee, Simon

Rhee, Lorenzo Lamas, Jay Leno, David Alan Grier, Sugar Ray Leonard, and many more.

Jun Chong made his dream into a reality and not only established one of the largest string of Tae Kwon Do schools in Southern California, but he also became the arts biggest advocate by promoting the arts through magazine covers, articles, books, and social media. For the last 55 years, he became a pioneer in spreading Tae Kwon Do to an American audience.

The Mother of Judo
Keiko Fukuda

Keiko Fukuda

BORN
April 12, 1913

DIED
February 9, 2013

BIRTHPLACE
Tokyo, JAPAN

PRIMARY STYLE
Judo

Many people throughout the world's history have made such an impact that their contributions will continue to be felt throughout time. Sensei Keiko Fukuda is one of those history-making individuals. She was so dedicated to her craft that it would be nearly impossible to come even close to what she has accomplished.

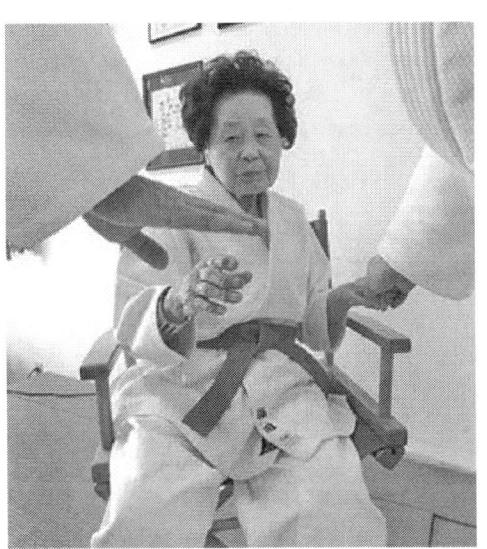

A Japanese-American martial artist, Keiko Fukuda became the spokesperson for women in the martial arts worldwide. Facing a male-dominated sport, Fukuda was not only the first female Judo instructor, but she was the first female to hold the rank of 10th dan, a feat that, to this day, no one else can claim.

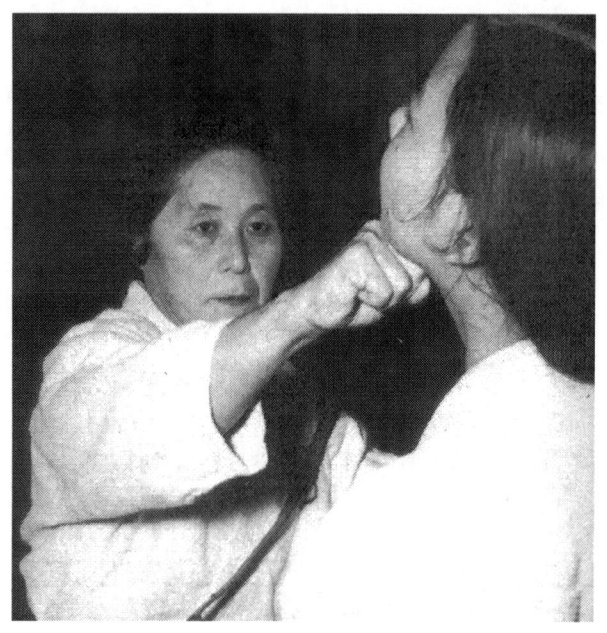		Fukuda was born in 1913 in Tokyo, Japan. Like most Japanese young women during that period, she took classes in flower arrangement, studied calligraphy and practiced the traditions of conducting the tea ceremony. But unlike her friends, her favorite pastime was listening to the stories about her grandfather: his time as a samurai and how he used martial arts skills to battle against his enemies. It was those stories that fascinated the young Keiko.

Hachinosuke Fukuda was her grandfather who happened to be a teacher in an artform called Jiu-Jitsu. History reveals that one day a young man came to the door to learn Jiu-Jitsu. The man was recommended by a fellow teacher, Sadanosuke Yagi. The young man's name was Jigoro Kano.

Sensei Fukuda accepted him into his school and taught him Yoshin-ryu and Shin No Shinto-ryu Jiu-Jitsu. Jigoro Kano trained with her grandfather for many years and became one of his finest students.

Over time, Jigoro Kano became close to the Fukuda family and he was treated like a son. They were very impressed with his dedication to the art and when Sensei Fukuda eventually passed away, the family asked Jigoro

Kano to become the art's successor and he agreed.

To further his studies, Jigoro Kano also studied Tenjin Shinyo-ryu under Masatomo Iso. Kano felt that many Sensei Fukuda's movements could be improved upon, and yet others moves he felt were unnecessary.

Jigoro Kano wanted to revamp the art into a sport and take out some of Jiu-Jitsu's more dangerous techniques. He wanted to improve his health and well-being using only certain aspects of Jiu-Jitsu. After many years of study and practice, he created a new artform he called Judo, which means "Gentle Way."

Kano relocated the school downtown to the Kodokan, hence the name "Kodokan Judo."

Many years later, Keiko's mother decided to visit Jigoro Kano at his new school and Keiko joined her. After all, Kano was like family to them.

The two watched the Judo players practice all evening, and Keiko was able to truly understand why her grandfather loved the martial arts so much.

Upon returning home, Keiko was convinced that she wanted to study Judo at the Kodokan.

After several months, Keiko went downtown to visit Kano's school to become his student. Even though most of the students were men, Kano was happy to accept women as students. In fact, he created a women's section at the Kodokan school. However, this situation was different as he personally welcomed Keiko to study Judo out of great respect for her grandfather.

The year was 1935 when Keiko Fukuda began her training. She wasn't alone as 24 other women showed up at the school that day wanting to learn Judo.

Keiko's mother and brother were very supportive of her decision to train in Judo, but her uncle was not pleased with the idea. Since Keiko was so shy, her mother and brother thought it would help her come out of her shell, and in time, she would marry one of the other Judo practitioners and discontinue studying the art.

Keiko Fukuda did the opposite and immersed herself in the art. She trained constantly and became one of the top students at the school. She spent so much time studying that she decided to focus on Judo rather than getting married, much to the displeasure of her mother.

In 1972, she and her classmate Masako Noritomi became the first two

women to reach the ranks of 6th Dan. In 2006, Keiko Fukuda became the first and only woman to be promoted to 9th Dan at the Kodokan.

In July 2011, Keiko Fukuda stepped into history by being promoted to 10th Dan in Judo, the highest degree in the art.

Over the years, Keiko Fukuda became the most outspoken and prominent leader for women in the martial arts. She later relocated to San Francisco, where she continued to teach until she died in 2013.

The First Judo Olympic Gold Medal Winner
Kayla Harrison

Kayla Harrison

BORN
July 2, 1990

BIRTHPLACE
Middletown, Ohio
USA

PRIMARY STYLE
Judo

Jigoro Kano believed that Judo would revolutionize the world, and for the most part, it did. Judo not only became listed as an official sport for nearly every school in Japan, but Judo was also practiced by an American president, Theodore Roosevelt.  Although Kano was part of the Olympic sports committee, he was never able to have Judo listed as an official Olympic sport.

Unfortunately, Kano died in 1938 and never enjoyed the impact Judo made when it appeared in the 1945 movie "Blood on the Son." The movie brought it national attention.

In 1964, Judo's popularity reached an all-time high when it became the first martial art to be a recognized sport in the Tokyo Olympics. America sent a team of their best Judo prac-

tioners to go against Japan's top champions. Although the American team put up a great fight, only one American competitor, Jim Bregman, came home with a bronze medal.

For nearly fifty years, no American has been able to capture a gold medal in Judo. That all changed when Kayla Harrison came along. It was in the 2012 Olympics, American Judo black belt Harrison stepped into history as she defeated Great Britain's Gemma Gibbons to win America's first Judo gold medal.

Men had been competing for the gold since 1964; there wasn't a category for women's Judo until 1992.

Not only did Harrison make history with the first gold medal ever awarded to an American, but four years later, she also went back and won the 2016 gold medal.

Harrison, born in Ohio, began her training at the tender age of six. Since her mother was already a Judo black belt, she probably learned how to flip an opponent before she could walk.

She began her formal training as a teenager, and she had won two na-

tional championships by the time she was 15. After facing a personal struggle at the gym, she and her family relocated to Boston, MA. There, she restarted her training with Sensei Pedro and his son Jimmy, a two-time Olympic Bronze Medalist.

The Pedro's welcomed her with open arms and became her surrogate family. Their training, discipline, and personal support helped Harrison fight through her emotional pain and transform herself.

For the next several years, Harrison became a dominating force in Judo competition. She won several different medals at the Junior World Championship and the World Judo Championships. Since the United States was unable to qualify for her division in the 2008 Olympics, Harrison set her sights on the 2012 games.

Unfortunately, before the 2012 Summer Olympics, Harrison injured herself while training and tore a medial collateral ligament. Though she had to readjust her training to avoid re-injuring her ligament, she continued preparing herself for competition. It was then that she stepped into history by becoming the first American to win a gold medal in Judo. It was then that the United States Judo Association promoted her to 6th Dan, the youngest to achieve this rank.

Kayla Harrison changed Judo forever and opened the door for a new generation of Judo practitioners.

Keeping the Hwa Rang Warrior Spirit Alive
Taejoon Lee

Taejoon Lee

BORN
May 17

BIRTHPLACE
Seoul,
SOUTH KOREA

PRIMARY STYLE
Hwa Rang Do

Taejoon Lee is a true example of a man who carries on the traditions of those before him. Son of icon and Hwa Rang Do founder Joo Bang Lee, Taejoon believes that it is not his goal to make better martial artists but rather, better human beings.

Serving as the vice president of the World Hwa Rang Do Association, he holds the rank of 8th-degree black belt, and throughout his lifetime, he became the biggest promoter for the advancement of Hwa Rang Do. Through numerous demonstrations, books, videos, and performances, Lee also applied his business knowledge into making Hwa Rang Do one of the most successful and loyal martial arts schools in the world.

Under the guidance of his father, Taejoon Lee grew up studying Hwa Rang Do even before he could walk. It didn't surprise anyone when he became the youngest in the system to earn his black belt.

The system of Hwa Rang Do began in the 1960s. Like many artforms during the rebirth of Korea after the Japanese occupation, the styles reflected some of the characteristics of Judo, Karate, Jiu-Jitsu and more. Founder Joo Bang Lee and Taejoon Lee were able to transform many of the Japanese tech-

niques into a modern methodology and draw on the spirit of the Hwarang warriors of ancient Korea. Hwa Rang Do doesn't just specialize in acrobatic and aerial kicking, it also blends a variety of movements such as joint-locking, throwing, grappling, striking, and a mix of unique weapons.

For example, Taejoon Lee took the Japanese art of Kendo, which had a more linear approach, and transformed it into a complete blocking, striking, and maneuvering system. It was no longer the Kendo of old, but a sword-fighting art that was more practical for today's society.

Bringing the art from Korea to America was another story. The arts of Tae Kwon Do and Hapkido had already been established in the United States, so it was up to Taejoon and his father to demonstrate the difference Hwa Rang Do had to offer.

Since Taejoon Lee was enrolled as a student at the University of Southern California, he felt it would be the ideal location for introducing Hwa Rang Do. First, he set up a number of demonstrations which led to Hwa Rang Do classes forming on campus. It wasn't long before he started launching a series of courses at UC Irvine, UC Riverside, UC San Diego, and Cal State Long Beach, which became the formation of the Intercollegiate Hwa Rang Do Society.

In 1994, Lee established the West Coast Headquarters of the Hwa Rang Do Association in West Los Angeles and later established the first Hwa Rang Do European Headquarters.

Taejoon Lee continues to transform Hwa Rang Do, yet keep the traditions of the Hwarang warriors alive for a new generation.

One of Karate's Greatest Pioneers
Tsutumo Ohshima

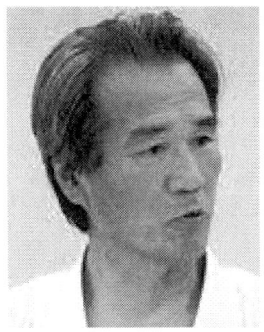

Tsutumo Ohshima

BORN
August 6, 1930

BIRTHPLACE
Nagasaki,
JAPAN

PRIMARY STYLE
Shotokan
Karate

Tsutomu Ohshima was born in Japan in 1930. By the age of five, he began studying the traditional art of Sumo. Sumo wrestling is an art of honor and great respect and it is considered one of the oldest forms of martial arts in Japan. A few years later, he was introduced to the art of Kendo, a form of samurai sword fencing. When Ohshima reached nine, he started learning the art of Judo.

One day, an event happened right in front of him that would change Ohshima's life forever. He was just 15 when he and his friend were on their way to Tokyo. They happened to come by a group of bullies picking on a classmate from school.

Ohshima knew the boy, he was only about 15, and he was shy and quiet and that's why they were attacking him. Ohshima said it made him very angry. Not just because of what was happening to the boy, he was mad at his friend,

who kept telling him, "Don't go, you'll get beat up."

Ohshima didn't do anything to help the boy. He admitted to himself that he was ashamed. He knew that this was an injustice but he couldn't convince himself to help him. He knew if he did, he would have been beaten up as well. Although he couldn't stand what was happening, he just stood there. He said to himself, "Alas. I am a coward."

From that moment on, Ohshima would question himself, "Am I ready to do something because I believe in justice?"

It was 1948, Ohshima was now 18 and attending Waseda University when he began his study of Karate. His teacher was Gichin Funakoshi, the actual founder of Shotokan Karate. Ohshima joined the university's Karate Club and became captain in 1952. The club had many of Funakoshi's students who helped him improve his training. Five years after he had begun training, Funakoshi awarded him third-degree black belt.

In 1955, Ohshima, now one of Funakoshi's instructors, decided to travel to America to continue his education at the University of Southern California. Two years later, he founded the first University Karate Club in America at the California Institute of America (Caltech). In that same year, Funakoshi awarded

him with his fifth degree.

In 1959, Ohshima stepped into history by creating the Southern California Karate Association (SCKA). For a few years, Ohshima returned to Japan to finish his university studies leaving Hidetaka Nishiyama in charge of the organization. He returned to America and grew the SCKA into the largest Karate Association in the nation, and renamed it Shotokan Karate of America.

Ohshima became a faculty member at Caltech as a physical education teacher. He wrote two books on Shotokan and translated Funakoshi's book into English.

Tsutomu Ohshima became one of the most prominent figures in martial arts history and the biggest advocate for Shotokan in America. With thousands upon thousands of students under his guidance, he continues to spread the art of Shotokan across the globe.

Stepping into the Lion's Den
Ken Shamrock

Ken Shamrock

BORN
February 11, 1964

BIRTHPLACE
Macon,
Georgia
USA

PRIMARY STYLE
Wrestling

The UFC. They are more than just initials for the Ultimate Fighting Championships; they are three letters that changed the face of the martial arts world forever. Although bare-knuckle fights, Kickboxing, and Muay Thai full-contact events were already taking place since the mid-1970s, the UFC would take the martial arts in an entirely new direction.

The Gracie Family, which had been holding Jiu-Jitsu-style full-contact events for years, was contacted by promoter Mike Davies and together, the formed the UFC. Initially, the UFC contest was very unorganized, and rules continued to change fight after fight.

    The UFC was a new frontier, and it took competitors who were both cunning and brave to enter "The Octagon" because no one knew what to expect. It was a free-for-all and the last man standing was the winner.

    Ken Shamrock was one of those brave fighters who dared to step into the ring. Shamrock, however, wasn't walking into the arena blindly; he was already a professional wrestler, a boxer, and a bare-knuckle fighter. It was then that Shamrock stepped into history by not only becoming one of the first fighters in the UFC, but he became one of its earliest champions.

With his "One-Punch Knock Out" reputation, Shamrock became a dominant figure in the ring. Called by many as the "godfather" of the UFC, ABC News named him one of the "World's Most Dangerous Fighters."

Because of its "brawl-like" appearance and lack of consistent rules, the UFC was being banned across the country. Senator John McCain and many others stood against the sport, while Ken Shamrock became an outspoken voice supporting it.

A powerhouse in the ring, Ken Shamrock had a tough childhood. Despite having parents, Ken grew up living in a Boy's Home. Over 600 boys were living there, and feuds were rampant. To settle their differences, it was either duking it out in the ring or wrestling it out on the mat. Ken got into many feuds, so he settled differences on a weekly basis. It wasn't long before he became the house champion and thus began his journey into the martial arts.

Ken Shamrock was a natural athlete who pursued weight lifting, wres-

tling, and football. When he was only 19, he entered his first "tough man" competition defeating an opponent outweighing him by sixty pounds. Outside the ring, he entered a number of organized street brawls and earned a reputation as "One Punch Shamrock."

When he got a little older, he worked as a bouncer but his father felt that his son was too talented for bouncing, so he suggested that Ken try his hand at professional wrestling. So, Ken decided to enroll in a wrestling academy and of course, became one of their most explosive students in the school.

Shamrock's friend saw his potential and introduced him to the UWF (Universal Wrestling Federation) in Japan. After a brief tryout in the states, he was on a plane to wrestle in Japan.

Unfortunately, his famous "one-punch" was ineffective against the advanced submission techniques, heel hooking, and arm barring used by champions Suzuki and Funaki; for Shamrock, it was a very humbling experience.

He was there to learn as he acquired these new skills very quickly. It wasn't long before he was able to successfully combat his Japanese peers. He became so good they even depicted him in comic books.

When Shamrock returned to the U.S., he opened a school for wrestling called the Lion's Den. It was the first official training academy for American Pancreas fighting.

One day, in September of 1993, Shamrock saw an ad in Black Belt magazine searching for experts to compete in a new event called the UFC; a bare-knuckle event with no rules. It was an ideal venture for Shamrock.

The UFC was an opportunity for Shamrock to fight various fighters, from Jiu-Jitsu practitioners to Kickboxers.

Shamrock stepped into history as one of the first successful competitors of the UFC. Using the tools he learned in Japan, Shamrock dominated the competition.

Shamrock continued with the UFC for a long career, becoming one of its greatest competitors, earning the first UFC Superfight Heavyweight Championship, and becoming a four-time UFC Heavyweight champion.

The Man Who Would Be King
Alexander Fu Sheng

Alexander Fu Sheng

BORN
October 20, 1964

DIED
July 7, 1983

BIRTHPLACE
Pok Fu Lam, Hong Kong
CHINA

PRIMARY STYLE
Tiger Crane Kung Fu

In the 1970s, Alexander Fu Sheng was Hong Kong's most gifted, talented and celebrated actors. Appearing in over 40 movies, Fu Sheng became the favored son of Chang Cheh, a legendary director for the Shaw Brothers.

The Shaw Brothers was Hong Kong's biggest movie production company. From fright films to period-piece Chinese Kung Fu movies, the Shaw Brothers were the guru's of martial arts movies. That was all about to change, however, when an American film called "Billy Jack" appeared in the

West. It was the first time that the martial arts played a primary role in a film. As a result, America fell in love with the martial arts and that's where a new page in martial arts history began.

As a result, the Western audiences began to hunger for martial arts movies and immediately, Shaw Brothers movies were now filling American theaters across the nation.

One of the darlings of the Kung Fu films was Alexander Fu Sheng. He had a certain boyish charm, a charismatic style, an impish nature with expert Kung Fu skills to match. In fact, he was the star pupil of iconic Kung Fu instructor Lau Kar-Leung.

Fu Sheng was unlike any other actor in Hong Kong. Although he played in a number of non-martial arts modern day films, he excelled in the Chinese period piece movies and it was there that his talents shined. He added a breath of fresh air to the Kung Fu revenge films by adding bits and pieces of comedy to his performances. With his boyish grin he would laugh at his opponent and one second later, strike him with a back fist.

Today, most people credit the comedic style of martial arts to Jackie Chan, but it was Alexander Fu Sheng who was the first to add his unique style of

comedy to martial arts movies and made him Hong Kong's favorite actor. Born Cheung Fu-Sheng in Hong Kong on October 20, 1954, he was the ninth child of a wealthy businessman. His family moved to Hawaii for several years and that's where Fu Sheng grew up and began his martial arts journey

137

learning both Judo and Karate.

Upon their return to Hong Kong, Fu Sheng decided that he wanted to  become an actor and his father enrolled him in the Shaw Brothers Southern Drama School in 1971. Fu Sheng was a natural and instantly drew the attention of one of Hong Kong's leading directors, Chang Cheh.

Chang Cheh knew talent when he saw it and assigned Lau Kar-Leung to train him in Kung Fu for the next six months. In less than one year of enrolling in the drama school, Fu Sheng was already featured as a leading role in the movie, "Police Force."

Just like that, Fu Sheng's career took off as he starred in such legendary films such as "Heroes Two," "Five Shaolin Masters," "Shaolin Temple," "Shaolin Martial Arts" and the "Brave Archer" series. Altogether, director Chang Cheh cast him in 23 of his films.

For the next decade, Alexander Fu Sheng was Hong Kong's biggest star and every movie he starred in, brought big numbers at the box office.

Along the way, he suffered a number of injuries such as his suspension wire breaking a falling eight feet and landing on his head. He also shattered

some bones in his right leg while working "Heroes Shed No Tears."

Sadly, at the height of his popularity, Fu Sheng's life was cut short as a result of an automobile accident. Fu Sheng was in the middle of filming "The Eight Diagram Pole Fighter."

Alexander Fu Sheng is considered responsible for re-inventing period-piece Kung Fu films. He was not only the first to add a spice of comedy to his role, but he became the face of the Kung Fu movie boom of the 1970s.

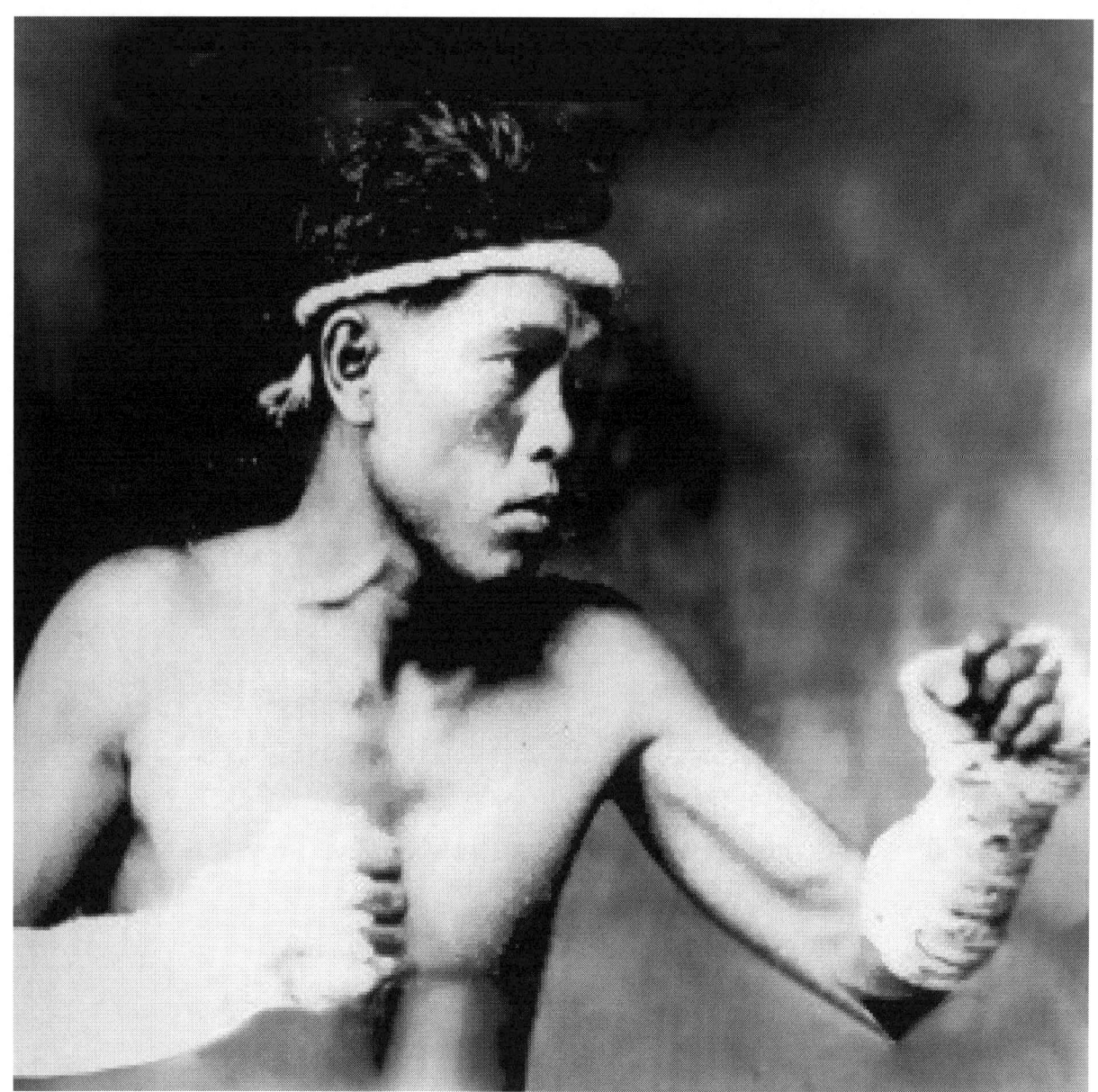

The Father of Muay Thai
Nai Khanom Tom

Nai Khanom Tom

BORN
Circa 1700s

BIRTHPLACE
THAILAND

PRIMARY STYLE
Muay Thai

Hide Nai Khanom Tom is considered a legend and folk hero for the people of Thailand. Athough he did not invent the martial art of Muay Thai, he became the art's greatest figure and is aptly called the "Father of Muay Thai."

According to most historians, the year was 1774, and Nai Khanom Tom was one of thousands of Thailand (then called Siam) prisoners that King Mangra of Burma was holding. The Burmese had just invaded Thailand's Ayutthaya Kingdom and captured them.

Just then, the Burmese were celebrating a special festival,

and the King wanted to have a match; his best boxing champion against one of the prisoner's best Muay Thai fighter. Nai Khanom Tom was the natural choice for the Thai as he was renowned for his Muay Thai skills and his never die attitude.

Note: Some stories say they weren't prisoners but met in a designated area, but either way, the two champions were ready for battle.

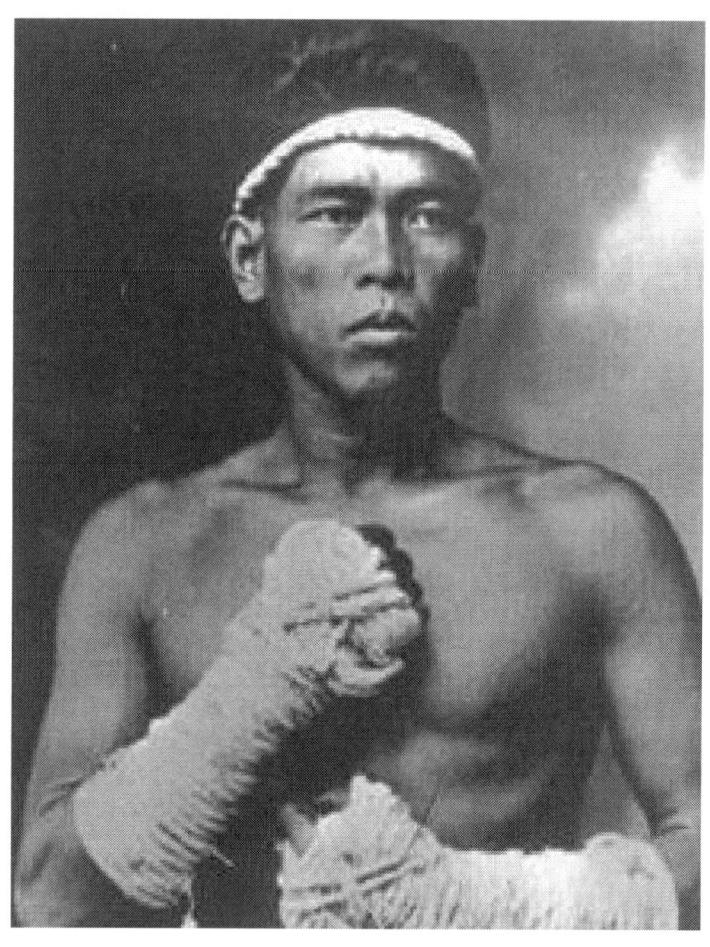

There were no rounds, no timekeepers, and they fought till one of them dropped.

Each fighter fought with their forearms strapped in hemp rope and bare-knuckled.

The Burmese fighter wore a traditional ankle-length sarong, and their fighting method focused more on their fists rather than the knees and elbows used in Muay Thai.

Nai Khanom Tom wore a loincloth wrapped around the body and tied in a knot. This gave him more freedom of movement and mobility.

Nai Khanom Tom fought for his King, his country, and the freedom of his people. His skills were too much for the Burmese fighter as Tom knocked him out.

A Burmese official said that their fighter was distracted by the Muay Thai music being played by the prisoners, so the King put another boxer in the ring to fight Nai Khanom Tom.

In total, the King sent in nine more fighters, one by one without a break between fights, and every one of them was knocked out by either a knee or elbow to the body.

King Mangra was the first to stand up and applaud the tremendous feat he had witnessed. He said, "Every part of the Thai

is blessed with venom, even with his bare hands he can fell ten opponents."

The King granted Nai Khanom Tom and all the prisoners their freedom.

Tom returned to Thailand for a hero's welcome. Defeating the ten opponents helped restore hope to the people of Thailand after their crushing defeat at Ayutthaya.

The legend of Nai Khanom Tom illustrates the best attributes of the art of Muay Thai. He symbolized a warrior willing to face all odds to defend his country and people.

For his feat, he is called the "Father of Muay Thai," and he is recognized every year on March 17th. Calling it "Boxer's Night," every stadium in the country dedicates its fights to Nai Khanom Tom's honor. It is the bedtime story for Thai children dreaming about legends and warriors protecting their King and country.

Bringing Wu Shu to America
Roger Tung

Roger Tung

BIRTHPLACE
CHINA

PRIMARY STYLE
Wu Shu

The date was February 21, 1972, when the United States President Richard Nixon landed in the People's Republic of China. It was the first time an American president visited the world's largest communist party while in office.

Nixon visited three of China's major cities and several historical sites while enjoying a variety of Chinese cultural performances. The visit softened many decades of diplomatic hostility and created a new course in the relationships between China and the U.S.

As a result, in 1974, the Beijing Wu Shu demonstration

team visited San Francisco to perform for President Nixon.

    Until then, most American martial artists had never heard of or seen Wu Shu. What they saw was a mouth-opening experience for traditional Kung Fu stylists. These Wu Shu stylists seemed to float across the air like flying dragons. Their movements were as smooth as silk, and the postures were lower and stronger than anyone could imagine. Watching these young people have movements that were so refined made traditional forms look like beginner techniques.

    Decades earlier, when the Communists took over China, one of the things they wanted to remove was traditional Kung Fu and the Shaolin Temple. To appease the government, traditional Kung Fu movements were made into more of a dance routine filled with acrobatic movements. The goal was to simulate the techniques rather than apply them.

The Wu Shu team toured a number of select places to perform. Many traditionalists sneaked their super 8 cameras into the venue to record their performance.

A year later, Roger Tung was one of those individuals from the Beijing Wu Shu team, who decided to move to America. Tung was not only a performer but an instructor as well. He opened the first American Wu Shu

facility in 1975 in Seattle, WA. Tung is one of three individuals that was regarded as bringing Wu Shu to America. The other two were Bow Sim Mark and Anthony Chan.

In order to bring more awareness to the art, Tung entered the American tournament circuit and dominated both the forms and weapons divisions for several years. Tung graced the cover of several magazines and countless articles. He also produced the first-ever Wu Shu instructional videos.

In 1981, Roger Tung, Anthony Chan and Bow Sim Mark organized the first-ever American Wu Shu team to compete in China.

Opening the Doors of Kung Fu to America
Dr. Kam Yuen

Kam Yuen

BIRTHDATE
March 10, 1941

BIRTHPLACE
Hong Kong
CHINA

PRIMARY STYLE
Tai Mantis Kung Fu

Unlike any other time in American history, the 1970s brought the most attention to the martial arts. One of these reasons for that attention was the debut of a television series that focused entirely on Chinese culture and tradition. Airing in 1972, millions of viewers were mesmerized as they watched the journey of a young half-Chinese boy who grew up in the Shaolin Temple and later fled to the American Old West after killing a member of the royal family. Called "Kung Fu," the TV series brought Chinese martial arts into the American living room as Kung Fu became a huge hit the day it aired.

But the show brought more than just a battle of Kung Fu vs. the gun-slinging cowboys of the

old West; it introduced America to the man behind the battle scenes. A man who was not only a technical advisor for the show's accuracy but a man who ensured the movements were correct and believable was Kam Yuen.

David Chow, a primary figure in the decision-making process of the series, was also planning on choreographing the fight scenes for David Carradine, the show's star, who had no prior martial arts training. Chow, however, was a Judo practitioner, not a Kung Fu stylist. That is when someone suggested that Kung Fu icon Kam Yuen join the production team and become its advisor.

Kam Yuen was more than just an advisor; he is one of the most highly regarded and respected teachers of Chinese Kung Fu. In fact, he is one of the earliest pioneers of Kung Fu in America and one of the first to open the doors to Asian healing methods and rejuvenation. Over the 60 years, he became the most successful figure in Kung Fu history, with many of his students becoming icons.

Born in Hong Kong, Yuen started his training with some of the finest teachers in the country, including Chen Zhen Yi and Tai Ji Tang Lang. They taught him the styles of Shaolin Kung Fu and Tai Mantis Kung Fu.

Upon moving to the United States, he continued training with several traditional Chinese instructors. One of them was Wong Jack Man in San Francisco, who taught him Northern style. Yuen also studied the arts of Tai Chi, Qigong, and Feng shui.

In 1965, along with classmates Paul Eng and Raymond Wong, together, they opened a school and formed the Tai Mantis Association. It was considered one of the earliest commercial Kung Fu schools in America. After four years of teaching, Yuen moved back to Hong Kong to further his study in Tai Chi with Chiu Chuk Kai.

When he returned to the United States, he was quite anxious to share his acquired knowledge of Tai Chi. He settled in Los Angeles, holding multiple classes at the YMCA, the Chinatown Recreation Hall, USC, UCLA, and Cal State L.A.

It was early 1972 when Hollywood came knocking on Kam Yuen's door. At the height of the Kung Fu movie boom, a new television series was about to debut. Kam Yuen was first called in to play Carradine's double, but his skills were so impressive that he was asked to serve as part of the crew. In fact, for several episodes, Yuen played a principal role on the show.

Yuen became Carradine's martial arts instructor and has been credited as the inspiration for the series' main character.

Through the years, Yuen authored a number of books, including "Be-

ginning Kung Fu," "Technique and Form of the Three Sectional Staff," the "Spirit of Shaolin, A Handbook of Kung Fu Philosophy," "Delete Pain and Stress On the Spot" (co-authored with Marnie Greenberg), "The Power of Instant Healing, Instant Rejuvenation" and "Instant Pain Elimination."

A doctor of Chiropractic, Dr. Yuen, now consults patients who suffer from chronic pain. His method was initially called Yuen Energetics, but it was changed to the "Yuen Method", co-founded with Greenberg.

Dr. Kam Yuen is not only a pioneer, but he opened America's eyes to Asian culture and tradition.

"2012 Funakoshi Award Winner"

Founder of the Martial Arts History Museum
Michael Matsuda

Michael Matsuda

BORN
March 6, 1959

BIRTHPLACE
North Hollywood,
California
USA

PRIMARY STYLE
Monkey Kung Fu
(Tai Shing Pek Kwar)

There has never been a museum dedicated to the martial arts…ever! Granted, there was once a Bruce Lee museum, sort of; it was just a section in a store in Los Angeles Chinatown that lasted for about a year. There have also been exhibits for Bruce Lee at various Asian history museums. There are also museums in Japan, China, and more that feature different

historical events that are connected with the martial arts. But, there has never been a museum that provides a historical look at martial arts until now.

The Martial Arts History Museum is an actual brick-and-mortar facility that has been in existence for 23 years. Located in the city of Burbank, CA, the museum has been keeping the flame of the martial arts alive. Lined with photos, historical facts, timelines, beautifully designed displays and historical

videos, it serves as a resource center for martial arts information and history.

The museum is the brainchild for martial arts veteran and historian Michael Matsuda. Matsuda was the publisher of Martial Art Magazine and former contributing editor for Inside Kung Fu and Black Belt magazine. An author of various books on martial arts history, he has been doing martial arts since 1967 and is still a teacher of Chinese Kung Fu.

The idea of the museum actually came in 1988. Matsuda had created a magazine whose goal was to focus on Asian culture and martial arts tradition.

The ads, which kept the magazine alive, were all tournament ads, so he had to shift the path of the magazine to primarily tournaments. It was all about tournaments for four years, which was not the original plan.

One day, a Karate artist named Bob McCauley offered to purchase the magazine and before he could finish his sentence; it was sold!

Matsuda first met with Douglas Wong to get his thoughts about a museum. Matsuda had great respect for Wong and listened to his advice. Wong felt that a museum is greatly needed and Matsuda should proceed with his plan.

    The museum first began as a touring exhibit as Matsuda borrowed nearly half of Wong's school to take on tour.

    At the same time, Michael did not want the museum to fail, so he went back to college for another 8 to 9 years to learn business design, marketing, public relations, directing, producing, and even filmmaking. He needed to know every aspect of running a museum.

    In 1999, the museum became official on paper and launched on the internet with the help of Fariborz Azhakh, who financed the website and paid for the construction of the tour display walls.

The Hall of Fame Inductees

2013

Lau Bun

Peter Cunningham

Alan Goldberg

James Hong

Mako Iwamatsu

Dave Johnson

Richard Rabago

Felix Roiles

Mark Shuey

Tino Tioulosega

FUNAKOSHI AWARD WINNER
Anna May Wong

The Father of Choy Li Fut in America
Lau Bun

Lau Bun

BORN
1891

DIED
1967

BIRTHPLACE
Toi San,
Guangdong Province
CHINA

PRIMARY STYLE
Choy Li Fut
Kung Fu

Trained privately by Kung Fu legend Yuen Hai, it was no wonder that his favorite student, Lau Bun, would eventually become one of the most skilled practitioners and accomplished teachers of the art of Choy Li Fut Kung Fu.

Lau Bun was born in 1891 in the city of Toi San in the Guangdong Province of Southern China. As a young child, Lau was introduced to the arts of Hung Gar, Mok Gar and several other Kung Fu styles. His father, who did very well financially, spent much his time away from home, so when he got a little older, his father arranged for the most famous Choy Li Fut style instructor in China to teach his son privately: Yuen Hai.

Sifu Yuen Hai's wife was also an accomplished teacher in

the Shaolin Five Animal system and taught Lau a variety of sword fighting forms. However, Lau was consumed by Choy Li Fut and became Yuen's senior student. When Sifu Yuen Hai passed, it was Lau Bun who became his successor.

In the 1930s, China was going through an uncertain time. Opium warlords began to take over the country, so the only means of escape was to immigrate elsewhere. Lau Bun decided to go to America by landing in Mexico and crossing the border.

To make a living, Lau served as a Chinese herbalist. In addition to teaching him Choy Li Fut Kung Fu, Yuen Hai also taught Lau Bun acupressure, the process of making Dit Dow Jow, and how to work with traditional Chinese herbs.

Although Lau Bun wanted to teach Kung Fu for a living, no one from the Los Angeles Chinese community had even heard of him, that is, until one day when an event occurred that changed everything.

Lau quarreled with an immigration officer in Los Angeles, and a patrol car arrived to arrest him, but he resisted the arrest. He took off, escaped into a building, and was pursued by four or five immigration officers. Eventually surrounded, Lau Bun fought his way out and ran into the streets of Los Angeles.

When the Chinese community heard about this, they named him the chief instructor of the Hop Sing Tong's Kung Fu club, teaching Choy Li Fut.

Through this, Lau Bun is credited as the first instructor to teach Choy

Li Fut in America. From 1931 to 1939, he established the Wah Keung Kung Fu Club teaching many Tong members Choy Li Fut.

Lau later relocated to San Francisco and was welcomed with open arms as he opened a school there where he taught traditional Lion Dancing and the art of Chinese herbal medicine to his students. It is said, Lau cured thousands of injuries. He was a very generous man as he gave continually every year to the Chinese Hospital in San Francisco.

When Lau Bun passed away in 1976, his senior student took over the studio, moved it to a new location, and renamed it the Hung Sing Studio. He appointed one of Lau Bun's youngest students, then only 19 years old, Doc-Fai Wong to be the head instructor.

His Kicks are "Sweeter than Sugar"
Peter Cunningham

Peter Cunningham

BORN
March 25, 1963

BIRTHPLACE
Port of Spain,
TRINIDAD AND
TOBAGO

PRIMARY STYLE
Kickboxing

Peter was born in the Port of Spain, Trinidad, and Tobano in 1963. At the tender age of six, his parents divorced, and his mother, Rosel, now the sole breadwinner for the family, moved to the small Island of St. Vincent in the West Indies, together with him and his siblings.

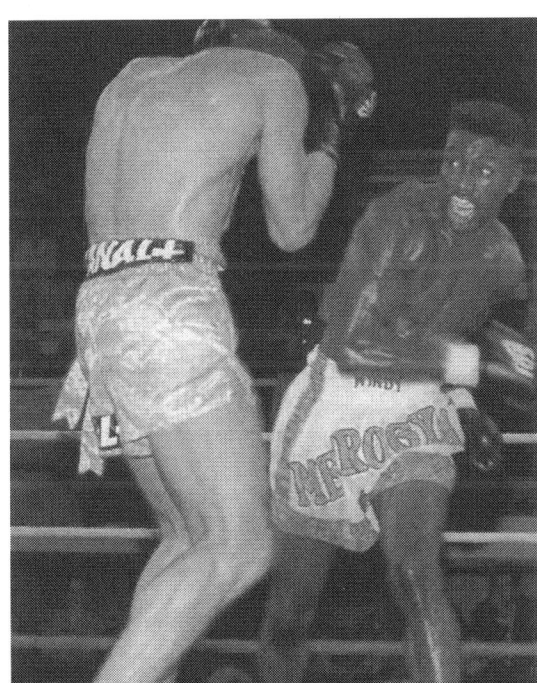

When Peter was 10, he saw "Enter the Dragon." It changed him forever as he noted, "I'm going to be like Bruce Lee."

Three years later, his family moved to Edmonton, Alberta, Canada. In 1978, while attending St. Marks Junior

High School, Peter enrolled in his first official martial arts class. The artform was Karate taught by Robert Supeene Sr. Cunningham immediately fell in love with the sport and went to the dojo every chance he got.

By this time, Kickboxing was in full swing, and people like Bill Wallace, Benny Urquidez, and Jeff Smith were making their marks in history, and Cunningham wanted to be part of that.

In 1980, Cunningham threw his hat into the Kickboxing arena in Canada: it was an amateur Kickboxing bout against Reg Johnson, which he easily defeated.

To improve his skill, Cunningham began boxing lessons with Ted James, and his son Rock at the South Side Legion Boxing Gym in Edmonton.

So excited about the sport, he fought several bouts in his first year of amateur fighting. Cunningham dominated his opponents the entire year. His friends from the dojo, who cheered him on at every fight, gave him the nickname "Sugarfoot." It was a combination of the names of two of the greatest fighters in boxing and Kickboxing. "Sugar" represented "Sugar" Ray Leonard, and "Foot" for Bill "Superfoot" Wallace.

In January 1981, Peter met the legendary Benny "the Jet" Urquidez, who was giving a seminar on Kickboxing. At the end of the workout, Urquidez told him, "you are going to be a great champion."

That gave him that extra confidence as "Sugarfoot" began his professional Kickboxing career. His first opponent was Canadian champion Gordy Gong. With a roundhouse kick to the head, Peter won by a kick knockout. Attending the match that evening was Ruben Urquidez, brother of Benny, and Blinky Rodriguez, brother-in-law to Benny.

They not only congratulated him on the decisive win but extended an invitation to train at Benny Urquidez's gym called the "Jet Center" in Van Nuys, CA. It was a dream come true for Peter, and he gladly accepted their invitation.

Cunningham soon packed his bags and arrived at the Jet Center to train. In addition to Kickboxing, his boxing skills were unsurpassed as he also entered a few boxing bouts. Returning home to visit his mother, he was featured on the undercard of boxing great Muhammad Ali's exhibition match in Canada.

Fighting against the World Lightweight Champion, Peter defeated him with lightning speed. His movements were so impressive that Ali's trainer, Bundini Brown invited him to train with them at the Joe Lewis/Muhammad Ali Gym in Santa Monica, CA.

For the next three years, he trained at both gyms nearly everyday. Peter excelled at both sports, but he began to gravitate towards Kickboxing after losing a controversial boxing championship bout. Cunningham focused

entirely on Kickboxing and quickly became a prominent fighter in the ring.

It was about this time that he stepped into history. As Kickboxing continued to grow, a new crop of fighters from Thailand began entering the American arena. They were using an artform called Muay Thai, which allowed for the use of elbows and knees, which they were quite proficient at. Many American fighters fell to the wayside as the Muay Thai fighters took advantage of their lack of exposure. That was until they went up against Peter.

With his dance-like movements from Ali and the power and strength he learned from Urquidez, Cunningham was not only able to go toe-to-toe with the Thai fighters, but he also became their worst nightmare.

For over 15 years, Peter Cunningham became one of the greatest fighters in Kickboxing history. With a record of 50-1-1, he retired as a 7-Time World Kickboxing Champion.

The King of Promoters
Alan Goldberg

Alan Goldberg

BIRTHPLACE
Brookyln,
New York
USA

PRIMARY STYLE
Wing Chun
Kung Fu

Alan Goldberg is undoubtedly one of the most successful entrepreneurs and event promoters in martial arts history. Founder of the Mega Martial Arts Weekend Event, it is an event that brings in thousands upon thousands of people

every year. Evolved over time, it has gone from a dinner and convention to a multitude of seminars, workshops, tournaments, and more. It is a place in which many of the greatest icons and prominent figures in the martial arts world have visited.

Despite being held in the middle of winter on the East Coast, Goldberg's Action Hall of Honor dinner ceremony is the height of the three-day weekend. With tables as far as the eye can see, the event averages between 3,000 to 5,000 attendees.

It all started around 2001 when a young Wing Chun Kung Fu Practitioner named Alan Goldberg launched the Action Martial Arts magazine publication. At the time, a flood of magazines was already on the newsstands, so Goldberg took a different approach.

He would send stacks of magazines to martial arts stores, schools, tournaments, and special events free of charge. The advertisements would pay for the publication of the magazines, but Alan paid for the mailings from his own pocket. It became a very wise choice on his part as it became an opportunity to promote future events.

Since it was free, Action Martial Arts magazine became one of the most sought-after publications. Within its pages, it covered special events, biographies, features, and the latest in martial arts news. The magazine was not only

a way to inform the public of different martial artists, but it created a name for the publication and opened the door for introducing the Mega Martial Arts Weekend Event.

After much advertisement and publicity in the magazine, when the first Mega Weekend became a reality, it became an immediate success. Held at the Atlantic Cities Tropicana Casino and Resort, the first dinner ceremony was called the "Hall of Honors," which brought in over 2,000 martial artists; this next year, they celebrate year 21.

Alan Goldberg, the founder, and organizer of the Mega Weekend, has been practicing the martial arts for over 55 years, beginning with the art of Shotokan Karate with Manard Miner and George Cofield. He would later study traditional Kung Fu learning the Five Animal system. In time, he met the man who would take him down a new path in the martial arts, Jason Lau.

Lau was a disciple of Jiu Wan, who studied with the famed Shaw Bros. Hong Kong production group. Jason Lau and Goldberg formed a friendship

that lasted for over 30 years. In fact, Goldberg spent five years living in a Shaolin Wing Chun temple with three other disciples. For Goldberg, it was a dream come true as they would wake up at two in the morning to train together.

Alan Goldberg eventually became one of the most respected teachers of Wing Chun Kung Fu in America and continues to share his art. Unlike so many before him who attempted dinner events or expos, Goldberg had the right ingredients, and even today, the Mega Weekend is the arts' most successful convention.

Creating a Path for the Next Generation
James Hong

James Hong

BORN
February 22, 1929

BIRTHPLACE
Minneapolis,
Minnesota
USA

PRIMARY STYLE
Various Artforms

There is no one like James Hong, nor will there ever be. In his 90s, he is the adorable father everyone loves in "Kung Fu Panda," one minute, then he's the evil Lo Pan in "Big Trouble in Little China" with death rays coming from his eyes and mouth, the next minute. Hong is the earth-shaker, the noise maker, the man that wouldn't take no for an answer.

It was actors like James Hong that paved the way for Bruce Lee, Jackie Chan, Jet Li, Tia Carrera, Kelly Hu and many more. It was Hong who not only just received his star on the Hollywood Walk of Fame, but he took the bull by the horns and changed Hollywood forever.

Since the silent film era of the 1920s, Hollywood blatantly discriminated against Asian actors. Even though many were highly gifted in their craft, Asian principal roles were given to Caucasians with makeup to resemble Asian "features." Actors such as John Wayne, Peter Lorre, and even Mickey Rooney all had significant roles that should have gone to an Asian actor.

Someone, however, had to hold their ground, and despite the negativity, despite the open discrimination, they would make their mark so huge, so big that it can be seen from the stars. One of those actors was James Hong.

Hong has done it all. From his role as Kato in the "Green Hornet" radio series to a wise Kung Fu master, he was able to break down doors to welcome a new generation.

Hong was born in 1929 in Minneapolis, Minnesota. His parents, Ng Fok Hong and Lee Shi Fa immigrated to America, first settling in Chicago and then moving to Minnesota, where his father owned a restaurant and was

part of the local Hop Sing Tong.

America was not an easy place growing up as an Asian child in the 1930s, so his family sent him to Hong Kong for the next ten years. He later returned to America to graduate from Minneapolis Central High School. His father was friends with the Peking Opera members visiting their town, so he allowed them to rehearse at the back of his restaurant. After watching them for some time, Hong became interested in the performing arts.

Hong moved to Los Angeles, graduated from the University of Southern California (USC), and worked as a civil engineer. In his free time, he enrolled in acting school with famed drama coach Jeff Corey.

Hong served in the United States military during the Korean war in 1950. Stationed at Fort McClellan and Camp Rucker, he would informally entertain his fellow soldiers. What started as doing a few comedy sketches for a small group of friends turned into an entire evening performances.

One day the camp general was in the audience and was so impressed, that he asked Hong to remain at Camp Rucker and be in charge of the camp's live show rather than deploying him overseas, which Hong believes, may have saved his life.

Upon returning to the states, Hong took his first step into show business when he was hired to redub soundtracks for several Asian films. This included characters on "Godzilla," "The Human Vapor" and many more, but a streak of luck helped launch his career.

One day, in 1954, Hong appeared on the radio/television game show "You Bet Your Life" hosted by Groucho Marx. During the show, he performed several impressions, including one of Groucho. Hong was a hit with the audience and got Hollywood's attention. All of a sudden, he was in high demand.

Altogether, James Hong has appeared in a principal role in over 650 films and television shows, and because of him, he created an opportunity for Asian actors worldwide.

Laying Down the Foundation
Mako Iwamatsu

Mako Iwamatsu

BORN
December 10, 1933

DIED
July 21, 2006

BIRTHPLACE
Kobe,
Hyogo
JAPAN

PRIMARY STYLE
Karate

The early days of Hollywood were especially difficult for Asian actors. Usually given small and insignificant roles such as a dishwasher or owner of a laundromat, many Asian actors were forced to speak with a heavy Asian accent to get a part, even though they didn't have one.

Makoto Iwamatsu, however, was a very different kind of actor. Like everyone else, he started with the minor, ac-

cent-heavy roles, but he developed into something different that somehow set him apart. There was something about him that people admired. Perhaps it was his low-tone, wise, and a bit majestic style voice? Maybe it was his

attitude toward the craft and his no-nonsense appeal?

Whatever the reason, Mako, as he referred to be called, was an extremely talented, versatile, and highly regarded performer. He moved from the tiny bit parts to landing leading principal roles that enabled him to bring a new dimension to his character. From a wise old teacher to a tortured soldier to a mangy sorcerer to a loveable cartoon figure, Mako continued to stretch the boundaries of his acting in every direction.

Many of today's youth may recognize his voice as the wise Uncle Iroh in "Avatar: The Last Airbender" television series. While others will know him from "Conan the Barbarian," Mako was able to transform himself and be considered by many as one of Hollywood's elite actors.

One of those reasons was his performance in the film "Sand Pebbles,"

which earned him an Academy Award Nomination for Best Supporting Actor as Po-Han.

Mako also appeared in a number of Japanese television dramas and films such as "The Bird People of China" and "Owl's Castle."

Mako's career included Broadway theater appearing in "Reciter," the "Shogun," the original 1976 productions of Stephen Sondheim's Broadway musical "Pacific Overtures" for which he was nominated for a Tony Award for Best Leading Actor in a Musical.

To support his fellow and upcoming Asian actors, Mako, along with six other Asian-American stars, formed the East-West Players theater company

in Little Tokyo.

Mako's presence in a film was undeniable. When his roles required martial arts skills, he looked to pioneer Tak Kubota for guidance and support. Although he did play a number of comedic roles and loveable characters, Mako took many of the roles that highlighted the martial arts. Some of these films included "Killer Elite," "Sidekicks," "An Eye for An Eye," "The Big

Brawl," "Bulletproof Monk" and many more.

Mako was born in Kobe, Japan, the son of a children's author and illustrator Tomoe Sasako and Atsushi Iwamatsu. His parents, who were actively voicing their opinion against the Japanese government, were considered political dissidents and had to move to the United States, leaving their son Mako in the care of his grandmother.

During this time, World War II broke out and since they settled on the East Coast, his parents were not forced to reside in the Japanese Internment Camps. In 1949, five years after the war with Japan ended, they arranged for Mako to join them.

Around 1950, Mako enlisted in the United States Army during the Korean War with the Special Services division performing plays for his fellow soldiers. It was then that Mako realized he had some natural acting ability.

Upon leaving the Army, he moved to Pasadena, CA, where he studied acting at the Pasadena Community Playhouse.

Actor Makoto Iwamatsu had a long film, stage, and television career spanning from 1959 to 2007. Altogether he is credited in over 160 roles.

The "Digital" Master
Dave Johnson

Dave Johnson

BORN
October 13, 1954

BIRTHPLACE
Dixon,
California
USA

PRIMARY STYLE
Tae Kwon Do

The internet. It was a term that was non-existent in the 1970s, and it was barely a whisper in the 1980s, but in the 1990s, everyone began to realize that the internet was going to be a significant part of our lives.

In the 1990s, another term called "E-Commerce" was coined as more businesses began posting their products for sale. People, however, were still hesitant to put their credit card information online for the world to see, but with new forms of security added, E-Commerce began to unfold in a big way, and it never looked back.

As far as the fitness and martial arts industry was concerned, another new door was about to open in the form of online training courses.

Money was no object for the fitness and exercise giants as they took advantage of a blossoming market and immediately set up their training courses. The martial arts community, however, was stumbling through it like three blind mice.

Granted, martial arts instructional VHS videos were already flooding the pages of Inside Kung Fu and Black Belt magazine, but delivering a course online was a whole new ballgame, and no one knew how to play.

That is until a businessman/martial arts instructor named Dave Johnson came along.

It was 1999, and Johnson was just finishing his master's degree in business, and the only thing he needed to complete was his thesis.

Since E-Commerce was only a few years old, his professor required his students to do their thesis on something related to online marketing, sales, or purchasing.

Dave Johnson was inspired. Over the years, he and many others had been purchasing instructional videos from companies like Panther Productions. Unfortunately, he could only see the videos when he could play them on a VCR.

Dave had the idea of creating a website that, for a nominal fee, would allow students access to a recorded instructor-led class that would be available on the internet 24 hours a day, seven days a week.

As the owner of two successful commercial schools in Central California, Johnson was aware of people's excuses for not working out. Some would say, "the timings not right" or "I can't afford the monthly fee," or "there are no schools near me to train." This idea was a long time coming, and until now, no one has done it successfully.

Simple enough? Not quite. Since Johnson's computer skills were lim-

ited, he sought out a computer company that was already familiar with the online training process. Unfortunately, as pointed out earlier, the internet was still new, and after paying two companies to create the program, he realized they had no idea how to make what he wanted.

It wasn't until he found a programmer named Greg Richburg of Netricks, Inc. that Johnson explained his idea of making a library of videos, and for a monthly fee, anyone could access them at any time on their computer.

Richburg knew exactly what Dave Johnson was looking for, and in just a few months, the world's first online martial arts training library was a reality. He even added special security encrypting as well.

Johnson not only stepped into martial arts history, but he received the highest honors for his thesis.

The Icon of Shorin-Ryu Karate
Richard Rabago

Richard Rabago

BORN
August 14, 1943

DIED
May 19, 2012

BIRTHPLACE
Oahu,
Hawaii
USA

PRIMARY STYLE
Shorin-ryu
Karate

For many years, the Japanese art of Judo was America's most popular form of martial arts. After all, it was an art form practiced by Theodore Roosevelt and, later, part of the Olympics. Karate, on the other hand, took a little longer to gain any form of recognition.

Even though the first commercial Karate school was already established in the mid-1940s, it would take another 20 years until people became more familiar with the art.

Richard Rabago became one of those early instructors to help pioneer Karate on American soil.

Born in 1943 on the Island of Oahu, Hawaii, Rabago was very fortunate because the Hawaiian Islands were the first stop for many Asian immigrants on the way to the Mainland. Some of those immigrants were martial arts instructors who happened to extend their stay on the Islands. As a result,

Rabago was able to study a variety of art forms, including Kung Fu, Aikido, and Jiu-Jitsu.

Furthering his education on the Island was very limited, so when Rababo completed high school in 1961, he moved to California to continue his education. It was then that the world of the martial arts became more accessible.

In California, Rabago met two of the most respected and highest ranking teachers in Shotokan Karate; Tsutomu Ohshima and Hidetaka Nishiyama.

It was an opportunity of a lifetime as he was accepted as their student.

The training was very traditional, very difficult and very strict, but it made for quality students. Richard Rabago studied at their school for over eight years, becoming one of their senior students.

California, however, was the melting pot for every unique style of martial art. So, in 1969, he decided to study the Japanese art of Kobayashi Shorin-ryu with sensei's George Terukina and Seikichi Iha. It was through Shorin-ryu that Rabago revealed that he had found his home as he remained

there for several decades.

It wasn't until the 1970s that Rabago set his site on promoting Karate across the world. He began by hosting seminars, writing books, appearing in magazines and talk shows, making appearances, and even opening his own Karate school to promote the benefits of Karate.

Richard Rabago became one of those early practitioners of Karate, studying under some of the most notable figures in Japanese art history. He was able to continue the values and teachings that made Karate one of the most revered traditional arts in the world. He became a spokesman and one of the biggest advocates for Karate for over three decades.

Keeping the Filipino Traditions Alive
Felix Roiles

Felix Roiles

BORN
October 20, 1975

BIRTHPLACE
Bongyas,
Catmon
Cebu
PHILIPPINES

PRIMARY STYLE
Pakamut
Filipino Fighting

To most of the Philippine society, Lapu Lapu is considered as the first Filipino hero because of his fight against the Spanish Empire as they sought colonization of their country. Lapu Lapu led the resistance and fought bravely against the Spaniards led by Ferdinand Magellan. He is heralded for his victory in the Battle of Mactan in 1521.

And so, it would seem fitting that an actual descendent of Lapu Lapu would continue his quest by preserving the Filipino arts. That someone

is Felix Roiles.

For the past three decades, Roiles has continued to promote the uniqueness of Filipino martial arts. He tries to preserve the traditional aspect of the art, the way he was taught by the elders of the Island. The same way it has been passed from generation to generation.

Roiles began his study in the Philippines when he was just a child and continued learning throughout his life. He was raised in the remote mountains area of Catmon, Cebu, by his grandfather, Andres Roiles. According to Felix, it was necessary to learn how to use any available tools to defend himself because there were many skirmishes in the mountains.

Felix practices the art of Pakamut, the original name of the Filipino

fighting art that originated in Mactan Island in the Province of Cebu. It is a tradition form of martial arts that reflects the Filipino people's history, philosophy, and culture.

Pakamut encompasses the Cebuano fighting style that utilizes impact weapons such as clubs, empty hands, and edged weapons. However, much of the focus is on sticks the blades like that of Kali and Escrima.

Over the years, Roiles has continued to bring awareness to the Filipino arts. In fact, for many years in both the Philippines and America, he participated in a number of tournaments including full-contacts matches as well. Roiles is listed as the four-time World Full Contact Stick Fighting Champion.

He placed 2nd at the World Eskrima/Kali/Arnis Championships and his Kali team defeated the rivals of 21 countries.

Roiles continues teaching the Cebuano fighting style in seminars and workshops worldwide. He teaches and coaches tactics to the military, and he has appeared in numerous magazines and even created his own system of weapons-making.

The Master of the Cane
Mark Shuey

Mark Shuey

BORN
April 19, 1947

BIRTHPLACE
Santa Monica,
California
USA

PRIMARY STYLE
Cane

One of the main reasons people take martial arts is because they were bullied in school, which is the case for Mark Shuey.

It was in the 4th or 5th grade that he was picked on and bullied. He recalls the bully started pushing him and hit him hard in the stomach. Young Mark was on the ground and

couldn't breathe. He remembers his friends just laughing at him instead of defending him or helping him out. Mark vowed it would never happen again.

Mark's father enrolled him in some Judo lessons, which only lasted a few months because the instructor had moved. But his best friend's dad was a Golden Glove fighter, and he taught his son John and Mark how to box and fight back using boxing in his garage.

At the time, kicking someone in a fight was not considered fair play, and one was labeled a cheater.

Mark Shuey continued learning boxing for quite some, and when he reached 7th grade, he got into a fight, and the outcome was very different.

With a little shuffle and a one-two punch, Shuey had beaten his opponent easily in front of the whole school. It was the last time he was ever picked on again.

Winning the fight encouraged him, and in fact, he began to enjoy physical sports such as wrestling, weightlifting, and gymnastics. Fighting was no longer a self-defense but a sport that he enjoyed.

Shuey and his friend Mark decided to look for a martial arts school and they choose one of Chuck Norris' Tang Soo Do schools in Southern California. After receiving his black belt, Shuey moved to Lake Tahoe. Learning that he was a martial arts black belt, one of the high schools asked him to teach the girls self-defense. Apparently, three of them had recently been attacked. Mark agreed, and even though he offered to teach for free, they refused and paid him regularly. It was his first teaching experience with up to 125 students.

Shortly thereafter, Shuey began his study in Hapkido and it was there he was introduced to a series of techniques that he could do with the ordinary cane. The Korean arts such as Tang Soo Do and Tae Kwon Do do not include any form of martial arts weaponry. The art of Hapkido, however, does include a small number of weapons. One weapon that has become more popular in many Hapkido schools has been the cane.

After several years of training, Mark Shuey became quite an expert in the cane. He was surprised to learn that no other systems specifically teach the cane.

Upon hearing about a violent attack against three elderly women who used two canes to fight off their attacker, it motivated Mark to take that step into history.

The traditional aluminum cane was too unpleasant to look at, and many seniors refused to use them.

Shuey figured that he would need to design a cane that would not only be pleasing to the eye but practical for fighting as well. Since serving as a general contractor at the time, Shuey was used to working with wood. So, with a bit of design and a whole lot of testing, he started making his own canes, and the Cane Master company was born.

To promote the cane, Mark Shuey began entering the Master's Weaponry division at a variety of tournament and took eight grand championships,

beating out the 20 and 30-year-olds.

As he started visiting senior citizen groups, he noticed that many were not strong enough to do much with the cane, so, he designed a complete exercise system to help get them strong.

Incorporating simple yoga movements to improve flexibility and easy exercise routines using the cane, many seniors were able to improve their wellbeing.

Over the years, Cane Master began adding a unique touch of artistry to every product. Some included the carvings of dragons, while others included cranes.

What started as a way to defend yourself, Shuey's Cane System developed into a health, fitness, rehabilitation, and protection program.

The Pioneer of Lima Lama
Tino Tuiolosega

Tino Tuiolosega

BORN
July 2, 1931

DIED
March 22, 2011

BIRTHPLACE
Island of Olosega
and Saposapoaluga
Feagaimaleata
Poumele Tuiolosega
SUMOA

PRIMARY STYLE
Limalama

Born into royalty, Tu'umamao "Tino" Tuiolosega was a member of the Samoan Royal Family and the son of the king of the Island of Olosega. As the Island prince, Tino was required to learn all aspects of Samoan traditions, including Polynesian dance movements. But unlike regular dance routines, they included a variety of secret techniques that involved kicking and striking.

Passed down from his grandfather Tagaloa Tuiolosega, it

was his father and uncle that taught him these hidden techniques. These particular movements were only reserved for those of the royal family line. As Tino progressed, his father and uncle advanced his training by introducing him to traditional Polynesian combat fighting.

When he came of age, Tino became part of the U.S military and participated in the Battle of Inchon. Tino Tuiolosega was so skilled that they asked him to serve as their hand-to-hand combat instructor.

In 1965, Tuiolosega stepped into martial arts history as he formed a new

martial arts system called "Limalama." The term "Limalama" is derived from the Samoan language, lima, meaning "hand," and malamalama meaning "understanding," also called the "hand of wisdom."

Limalama is a mixture of street fighting techniques and boxing movements. It is a more comprehensive self-defense system that anyone can understand. The art utilizes a number of circular movements which incorporates pressure points, knife techniques, boxing, Chinese Kung Fu, Japanese arts, wrestling holds, takedowns and locks.

Over the years, Tuiolosega traveled throughout the country, meeting and training with some of the arts' greatest icons, including Ark Y Wong and Edmund Parker. He is

considered one of the few non-Chinese to learn the art of Kung Fu.

Tino was also an acclaimed amateur boxer, fighting in over 100 matches. He combined a number of additional movements, such as from the art of Lua, into the Limalama art made it more effective.

Limalama was introduced to the world in a commercial school that Tuiolosega opened to teach the art in Hawaii. Later the art expanded to the mainland and throughout Mexico as well. According to present-day accounts, there are over 50,000 practitioners in Mexico, making it one of the most popular forms of martial arts there.

Referred to by many as the "Father of Modern Self-Defense," Tuiolosega formed the Limalama Association with several other martial arts figures, including Richard Nunez, John Marolt, Sal Esquival, Solomon Kaihewalu, and Haumea "Tiny" Lafiti, his cousin.

Tino Tuiolosega persevered the traditions of those before him so that it could be passed on to a new generation. He left the world too early, but his legacy will live on forever.

"2013 Funakoshi Award Winner"

The Pioneer, the Icon, the Legend
Anna May Wong

Anna May Wong

BORN
January 3, 1905

DIED
February 3, 1961

BIRTHPLACE
Los Angeles,
California
USA

Anna May Wong became the forerunner for not only every Asian actor, but opened the doors of opportunity for all minority actors worldwide.

With her career primarily in silent films, Wong became

one of the most prominent figures in Hollywood as a leading actress. Altogether, she appeared in over 60 films, 40 of which were silent.

The early 1900s were extremely difficult for immigrants, especially those from Asia. Interracial couples, including those in the motion pictures, were forbidden. Citizenships were denied, and the combination of the Chinese exclusion act and subsequent laws, Asians were practically banned from coming to the United States.

Anna May Wong, along with Japanese actor Sessue Hayakawa, were extremely talented actors during that time, and they used any influence they could to change the Hollywood stereotypes of Asian actors. Over time, Wong became the biggest advocate for change.

Anna May Wong was born Liu Tsong Wong in 1905 in Los Angeles, CA. The second of eight children, her family was originally from Taishan, China. In 1848, when gold was discovered in Northern California, her grandfather moved to America and opened a general store nearby.

After her grandfather died trying to save a woman who fell down a well, the family relocated to Los Angeles, CA, where they opened a laundry mat. It was one of the few options available to Chinese Americans.

The family lived in a diverse neighborhood as Anna attended the public elementary school. Since there were only a small number of Asians in school, she and her sister were constantly laughed at and bullied by the other kids. Anna noted that they would surround them, push them, pull their hair, slap her face and call her offensive names like "chink".

Hearing this, their father had them transferred to the Chinese Mission

School in Chinatown, where they were welcomed.

Wong worked for her father at the laundry mat, and any tips she earned while making deliveries, she used to buy movie tickets as she was fascinated by them. When many of the film production companies began relocating from New York to Los Angeles, Wong often skipped school to watch how they made movies. It was then, at the age of nine, Wong knew that one day she would become a movie star.

In 1919, after combining her English and Chinese names, she was cast as an extra in a film, "The Red Lantern." Her only scene was carrying one of the lanterns, but it would be her first step in a fantastic career. It was then that she began calling herself Anna May Wong.

That same year, she landed a role as the leading actor's wife in

"Bits of Life." At just seventeen, she dropped out of school to pursue acting. One year later, in 1922, she landed her first leading role in "The Toll of the Sea."

This became her big break as she began to take on bigger roles. In fact, she actually developed a following of fans.

Although there were many new doors open for Anna, she was either cast as a dragon lady or a murderous villain. Since there were laws preventing interracial couples in the movies, she could not play a character in love with a non-Asian actor.

To improve her career, in 1928, Wong accepted an offer to play a starring role in a European film. It was there that she excelled, working in Germany, France, and England. She began appearing on the cover of magazines as she became close friends with many American artists living abroad. It was there she learned to dance and sing on stage. Although many new principal roles opened up for her, periodically, she was cast as an "Oriental" character.

Wong's career soared for the following decade as she was even seen on American billboards and posters. She also created a documentary during her visit to China and raised money for many of the Chinese refugees during World War II.

Anna May Wong made such an impact that she changed history forever and created a path for others to follow.

The Hall of Fame Inductees

2014

David Carradine

Chan Sau Chung

John Lem

Al Leong

Charles Lewis

Chuck Liddell

Jeff Smith

Chuck Sullivan

Chen Kwan Tai

James Wing Woo

FUNAKOSHI AWARD WINNER
Osamu Tezuka

He Changed the World Forever
David Carradine

David Carradine

BORN
December 8, 1936

DIED
June 3, 2009

BIRTHPLACE
Los Angeles, California
USA

PRIMARY STYLE
Tai Mantis Kung Fu

October 1972, ABC Studios aired a new and unique television series called "Kung Fu." In less than a year, it became the number one show on American television, drawing a regular audience of 28 million viewers. Piggybacking off the Kung Fu movie boom dominating Western theaters, Kung Fu became the most popular show of the early 1970s, receiving widespread critical acclaim.

But Kung Fu was more than just a television show; it gave the world a glimpse of traditional Asian culture and tradition as it was in the late 1870s. Although Bruce Lee, who appeared as

Kato in the "Green Hornet," first introduced the Chinese arts on television, Kung Fu opened the door into the Shaolin Temple, the birthplace of Kung Fu.

Created in America, Kung Fu is an action/adventure drama filled with martial arts action, Taoist philosophy, and the relationship between a Shaolin Monk and his favorite pupil. It starred David Carradine, son of veteran actor John Carradine, as Kwai Chang Caine. Caine is the son of an American, Thomas Caine, and a young Chinese girl named Kwai Lin.

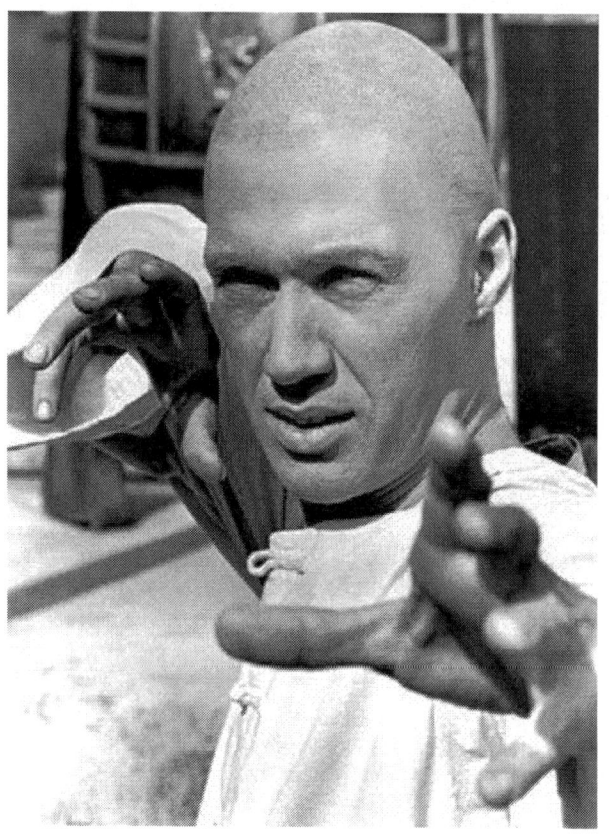

Raised by his grandfather in China, a young Caine seeks to be accepted into the local Shaolin Monastery after his grandfather passes away. After much consideration and testing, Caine is accepted into the Temple where he learns the ways of the monks, which includes learning the art of Kung Fu.

In the pilot episode, Caine's beloved elder and mentor, Master Po, is murdered by the Emperor's nephew. Caine is so upset and outraged that he

retaliates by killing the nephew. Wanted, Caine flees to the American Old West with only a knapsack of memories.

Armed with just his wits, his wisdom, and his Kung Fu, Shaolin monk Caine seeks to find his only relative, his half-brother Danny Caine. The show is filled with flashbacks of his Shaolin training and teachings while confronting nearly every bad guy in the West.

Carradine, who had been acting professionally ten years before Kung Fu and was groomed in acting by the entire Carradine family, actually pulls it off as a half-Chinese monk. In each episode, he teaches philosophy while he "fights like ten tigers."

In reality, David Carradine had no knowledge of Chinese Kung Fu or any other martial arts for that matter. However, Warner Bros. brought in Kung Fu expert Kam Yuen as a choreographer/technical advisor and on-site teacher for Carradine. Yuen is also featured in the series.

Although the series only lasted 63 episodes, which equals to about three years, it had a huge effect on the world and as a result, many people decided to study martial arts.

As a result of the Kung Fu series, Carradine's career continued to grow; however, nearly every role after that involved martial arts. Even as an assassin squad leader, he played the flute just like in the Kung Fu episodes.

The Legendary "Monkey King"
Chan Sau Chung

Chan Sau Chung

BORN
May 6, 1934

DIED
February 7, 2020

BIRTHPLACE
Hong Kong,
CHINA

PRIMARY STYLE
Monkey Kung Fu
(Tai Shing Pek Kwar)

Born Standing around five feet tall, Chan Sau Chung is regarded as one of the most powerful and respected teachers of Kung Fu in Hong Kong. Referred to as "The Monkey King,"

Chan Sau Chung was the final student and successor of the art called Tai Shing Pek Kwar or better known as Monkey Style Kung Fu.

Protégé of the great Ken Tak Hoi, Chan Sau Chung was one of only a handful of individuals who was considered a master of this rare and secretive Chinese martial art.

He is credited as the first individual to open the doors of Monkey Style Kung Fu to the American audience and the biggest advocate for the art during the 1970s.

Growing up, Chan Sau Chung had a difficult time in school. Since he was much smaller than the other kids, he was an easy target as the taller kids would tease him and beat him up.

When he was 12 years old, he and his two brothers started learning Kung Fu from one of the greatest teachers in Hong Kong, Ken Tak Hoi. The training was hard and difficult for his two brothers, but Chan Sau Chung had a natural talent for the art. Ken Tak Hoi first taught them Pek Kwar (Axe Fist) style but focused most of his teachings on self-defense to protect themselves. According to Chan Sau Chung, street fighting was very common in those days.

After just a year of training, Chan came face-to-face with one of his bullies. The boy was over a foot taller and was 20 pounds heavier than him. But this time, he wasn't going to let the bully get the best of him. Applying everything that he had learned, Chan Sau Chung was able to take down his adversary in just ten seconds. It happened so fast that Chan believed it was almost like magic.

That was the moment that changed his life forever. It proved to him that even with his smaller size and stature, Kung Fu worked. The fight encouraged him and put a desire in him to excel in Kung Fu. From that point on, Chan was in class every day.

For the next four years, Chan immersed himself in the art and, as a result, grew great respect from his teacher. In fact, Ken Tak Hoi decided to make him a full-time teaching assistant.

After completing his training Pek Kwar, Ken felt that he was prepared to learn the advanced art of the system, Monkey Style Kung Fu (Tai Shing).

Ken Tak Hoi believed that his students must first master Pek Kwar before learning Monkey. He felt that Chan had the perfect body type for Tai Shing.

Ken Tak Hoi allowed four of his top students, the very best that he had, to become part of his closed-door class. Chan was the youngest of the group, only 22 at the time. In the class, they would be taught the complete art of Tai Shing, including the five monkey forms and the monkey staff.

Chan Sau Chung continued his training for over 30 years with Ken Tak Hoi, and when his other three classmates passed, it was up to Chan to carry on the art to a new generation.

To further promote the art and bring it worldwide attention, Chan Sau Chung sent one of his top students to compete in the first Southeast Asia tournament in a full-contact bout. He achieved five straight wins and became the Middleweight Champion.

As a result, there was greater interest in Monkey Kung Fu. Chan was then invited to perform several demonstrations of the art, which brought him much notoriety. His student, Chen Kwan Tai, also became famous by being asked to star in several Hong Kong movies.

In 1974, Chan Sau Chung was invited by Buck Sam Kong to perform in the United States. The air was filled with excitement as Chan Sau Chung performed on stage. He not only performed Monkey Kung Fu movements, but he also demonstrated a little of the "drunken monkey" form.

Chan Sau Chung's popularity continued to grow as he continued to open the doors of Monkey to the West. He sent many of his top students to fight in a number of full-contact bouts in which they all returned victoriously.

Chan Sau Chung became the biggest spokesman for the art and was the first individual to bring awareness to the art worldwide.

The Hero of Choy Li Fut
John Lem

John Lem
(Chung Wong Lem)

BORN
July 20, 1922

DIED
January 23, 1999

BIRTHPLACE
CHINA

PRIMARY STYLE
Choy Lee Fut Kung Fu

John Lem was a practitioner of Choy Li Fut Kung Fu. It is an art form with many of its strikes based on long arm movements. Born in a small village in China, he grew up learning Kung Fu when he was just a boy.

Around 1970, John Lem opened a Choy Li Fut Kung Fu school on Melrose in Los Angeles. He is less than a handful of people who are considered a pioneer for bringing Kung Fu to America.

Lem was a no-nonsense kind of teacher. He was completely old school, but yet he was very traditional at the same time. He was short,

stocky, with arms and shoulders that were full of power. The training was more in the full-contact style. It was more like combat Choy Li Fut where every strike had to count. They only did a few forms as most of the training classes were hard, powerful, and tough.

He believed that Kung Fu should be kept private and not publicized. It was to be a private matter, and no one should know you are learning martial arts, lest they team up against you to outmatch one's skill.

In all the years running his school, John Lem never wore a "traditional"

Kung Fu uniform or sash when he taught. Students wore just a t-shirt with the school's logo and black workout pants with three white stripes like inverted "V"s.

Jerry Lem, John's son, recalled that he started training with his dad in their backyard before they had the school. His father used the lines in the concrete to check their stances and footwork. They also used the old fence to stretch his leg before going into his kicking drills. They used Japanese makiwara boards for striking, and they would fill a 50-pound Farmer John lard drum with sand for hand toughening; very low budget but it worked.

Rain or shine, it didn't matter to John Lem as he continued to teach his son. Jerry recalled many an afternoon they spent in the pouring rain practicing Kung Fu.

John Lem produced a number of highly skilled students who could handle his combat method of teaching. Jerry recalls one particular student who later became well-known doing another artform, couldn't handle the power movements, so his dad told him that this style was not suitable for him. He should go down the street and study at the Shaolin school instead.

Even though Kung Fu was being taught in America, before the Kung Fu movie boom, it was usually at community centers or YMCA's, and it for someone to have their own school, like John.

John Lem was a pioneer of Kung Fu in America. He provided an opportunity to look at Kung Fu in a more street-like manner, and he felt it providing his students with a more practical approach.

The Kwan Do Warrior
Al Leong

Albert Leong

BORN
September 3, 1952

BIRTHPLACE
St. Louis,
Missouri
USA

PRIMARY STYLE
5 Animals Siu Lum Kung Fu

By the 1970s, Kung Fu was all over the place. Period piece Kung Fu movies filled the theaters; there was a song called "Kung Fu Fighting," topped off by a highly successful TV series called "Kung Fu."

Although Kung Fu was spreading its way across the nation, the only place that it had very little attention was the tournament circuit. In an event filled with Karate and Tae Kwon Do judges, Kung Fu was misunderstood, and it was even listed as "Soft Style."

A few things, however, happened along the way to change everything.

First, it was Al Dacascos; he was a Kung Fu man in a

black outfit with arms that moved like windmills. He began entering forms and weapons but received low scores because the judges didn't believe it was effective. So, Dacascos traded in his weapons for a chance as a point fighting and cleaned a few Karate clocks along the way.

Immediately following was Eric Lee. A lone black uniform in a sea of white Karate gis. He quickly dominated the forms and weapons division and earned the title the "King of Kata."

It wasn't long until a new group of warriors appeared on the tournament circuit under the umbrella of Douglas Lim Wong's Siu Lum team. Headed by team co-captains Al Leong and James Lew, the Siu Lum demonstration team began dominating the forms and weapons divisions at every event.

According to Wong, the team still struggled with low scores from the judges because they didn't understand Kung Fu, but it didn't take long to convince them how powerful Chinese Kung Fu really was.

While James Lew focused on the creative kata, Leong wowed audiences

using a Chinese long weapon called the Kwan Do. Unlike today, when weapons are lightened for competition, Leong chose one of the heaviest weapons in Kung Fu.

Douglas Wong worked with Leong to add that extra spice to bring the traditional Kwan Do form to life. By providing additional twirling, lightning speed striking, and phenomenal acrobatic movements, Leong became one of the most dominant figures on the tournament circuit.

Leong and his team won so much that no one wanted to compete against them; the promoters began asking them to demonstrate instead.

Albert Leong began his martial arts journey in junior high school with Kung Fu legend Ark Yuey Wong. Wong is considered the "Father of Kung Fu in America."

It wasn't long until he met Douglas Wong, who was the head of the Siu Lum

school in Van Nuys. Douglas Wong was also a student of Ark Y. Wong. Douglas asked Leong to join his school to assist him in teaching.

Through the years, more doors kept opening for Leong as he performed countless demonstrations to promote the Siu Lum school. He appeared on numerous magazine covers, and it wasn't long until he began a career as a stuntman and actor.

Although he earned a reputation as one of the evil henchmen in Hollywood blockbuster films, it was his years as one of the nation's top competitors that changed history.

The Man Behind the Tapout Brand
Charles Lewis

Charles Lewis, Jr.

BORN
June 23, 1963

DIED
March 11, 2009

BIRTHPLACE
San Bernardino, California
USA

PRIMARY STYLE
Brazilian Jiu-Jitsu

Charles Lewis Jr., aka "Mask," was one of the most unusual yet flamboyant individuals in the industry of the martial arts. He wasn't a competitor, he wasn't a martial arts movie star; he was only a blue belt in Brazilian Jiu-Jitsu with a bit of training in Tae Kwon Do, but Mask made such a huge impact that he

played a major role in helping keep the Ultimate Fighting Championships (UFC) alive.

Mask was an entrepreneur and a businessman; he became a promoter, and he established himself as an entertainer who founded a clothing line called "Tapout" that not only made him super rich, but it provided an opportunity to further develop a sport that he truly loved.

Mask served his country as a United States Marine. After leaving the armed forces, he became part of the San Bernardino County Sheriff's Department. However, everything changed for him in 1993.

In November, Art Davie established a new form of no-holds bar competition called the UFC. Bringing in fighters from every discipline, it was a no-rules and winner take all match. The championships began with a bang as teeth were flying into the audience. It also served as the formal introduction of Brazilian Jiu-Jitsu as Royce Gracie became its first champion.

Mask was hooked and knew mixed martial arts would one day be his destiny. Mask believed in what mixed martial arts fighting was all about as he and a few friends enrolled in the Gracie Academy.

After reaching his blue belt level, he was already teaching submission techniques to the other officers who needed to learn some new moves in taking down confrontational prisoners.

Mask's father and mother were both giving individuals. His mother was a vice-principal at his school, and his father was a football coach. Both were highly respected because of the time they gave to troubled teenagers. Mask carried that same mentality throughout his life.

Mask decided he wanted to create something that would help further promote and bring attention to mixed martial arts. He felt it needed something to bring more depth to the sport.

In 1997, he decided to brand mixed martial arts with a unique clothing line called "Tapout." He expressed that the phrase was not about giving up as in a Tapout but making the other opponent submit with a Tapout.

With very little money for an investment and the help of a few friends, the Tapout logo was printed on t-shirts, stickers, and other forms of clothing.

Mask would pack the shirts into his car and head for the nearest mixed martial arts event. There, he would set up a little table in the parking lot and begin selling his wares. Unable to

afford a vendor fee, he would pack up his stuff whenever security came to chase him out.

Taking a leave of absence from his work and living with friends and sometimes in his car, Mask continued pushing his brand, and it wasn't long until he started making a little cash.

However, with every dollar earned, he reinvested into the fighters. The money came in to print the shirts, and out it went to sponsor an up-and-coming fighter. It was people like Chuck Liddell who were struggling to get by, and it was the Tapout brand that was there to help him.
As the business grew, the Tapout brand did whatever it could to help promote the sport, including placing thousands of UFC flyers in all of their shipments and sponsoring young fighters.

Since Mask was very shy, he created a character persona that would help him overcome his shyness. Putting stripes of face paint on himself and wearing a top hat, Mask created a more outgoing individual that everyone seemed to enjoy.

Ten years after establishing the Tapout brand, the company was making over $22.5 million dollars.

Through the good times and the bad, Mask was able to make a difference, and when it looked like the UFC was going to close, it was Mask who joined the fight to keep it alive.

Although his life was cut short, Mask became the only non-MMA fighter inducted into the UFC Hall of Fame.

The Face of the UFC
Chuck Liddell

Chuck Liddell

BORN
December 17, 1969

BIRTHPLACE
Santa Barbara,
California
USA

PRIMARY STYLE
Hawaiian Kempo Karate

It was in 1993 that a new sport was introduced that brought worldwide attention to the martial arts; calling themselves the Ulitmate Fighting Championships, the UFC opened pandora's box, and mixed martial arts was officially born. The event was a no-holds-barred competition held in Colorado and broadcasted live on pay-per-view; it was such a big hit that the word mixed martial arts immediately became part of the American vocabulary.

    Started by Art Davie, the Gracie family was heavily involved as Royce Gracie became its first champion. But the UFC became a life unto its own pitting champion against champion and style against style. Although many fought in the "Octagon," there was one man who quickly made a name for himself.

    Chuck Liddell, fighting under the name of "Iceman," has been widely credited for bringing mixed martial arts into mainstream American sports

and entertainment. Was it because of his unusual mohawk haircut, or was it his eye-piercing stare, or perhaps his ability to crush his opponent in seconds, Chuck Liddell's face that would become synonymous with the sport.

Although Liddell didn't step into the UFC Octagon until 1998, he was active in sports all his life. He played on the school's football team for four years straight in high school. At Polytechnic State University, he was a Division 1 wrestler.

Chuck began his martial arts training at 12 in Koei-Kan Karate. That was

 until he saw the art of Kempo Karate demonstration, and he knew he would follow Kempo for the rest of his life. The school was nicknamed "The Pit" and it was run by John Hackleman. Hackleman was one of the individuals responsible for accelerating the art of Kickboxing in the 1970s.

Hackleman's style was based on natural fighting techniques and conditioning. Liddell enjoyed studying Kempo so much that he even has a tattoo of Kempo on his shoulder.

At the time, Kickboxing was the most popular art for full-contact fighting as Hackleman groomed his student to compete. In fact, Hackleman gave him the name "Iceman" at his third kickboxing bout because Liddell's pulse rate rarely went up or down. While others had jitters before a fight, he looked like he was going for a stroll in the park. Hackleman remarked, "You have ice in your veins."

When Liddell made his debut in UFC 17, five years after the UFC began, he was an immediate powerhouse in the ring. Winning his first match

against Noe Hernandez. His next match, however, wasn't a UFC fight but rather an International Vale Tudo Championship, which was bare-knuckle, which he also won.

Liddell also fought with the Pride Fighting Championships, and it wasn't long before he became the UFC Light Heavyweight Champion. In 2007, he became the first UFC fighter on the cover of ESPN magazine.

His fighting career spanned over 20 years with a record was 21 wins with 9 losses. Although Liddell fought around the world for several different leagues, it was the UFC that gave him the most notoriety.

Pioneering Full-Contact Karate Fighting
Jeff Smith

Jeff Smith

BORN
March 4, 1953

BIRTHPLACE
Sedalia,
Missouri
USA

PRIMARY STYLE
Tae Kwon Do

Korean martial arts instructor who migrated to the United States in the early 1960s became the first individual to open a Tae Kwon Do school in the West. Though no one had even heard of the term Tae Kwon Do, a young Jhoon Rhee would put all of his marketing skills to work focusing on the college-aged crowd and it worked. From demonstrations to performances to self-defense classes to special events, Rhee was able to

daily.

That is until one day, while on his route, he saw signs posted on the campus bulletin board. The sign noted that there was going to be a karate demonstration at the student union ballroom.

Smith attended the event and was amazed at what he saw, and by the time the demonstration was over, he wanted to enroll.

There was, however, only one problem, the club was for college students only and Jeff was still in high school. He did his best to convince his mother to talk to the Dean to see if they could let him in. His mother was not pleased with him being so young, but after some convincing she met with the Dean and they decided to let Jeff and some of

open four martial arts schools in Virginia, Maryland, Washington, and Washington, D.C., mostly filled with college students.

Rhee, who would later be called the "Father of Tae Kwon Do in America," regularly traveled to each of his schools, some of which extended to other states by establishing dozens of college campus martial arts clubs. One of these campus clubs happened to be located at Texas A&M University.

Jeff Smith, only a teenager then, had a part-time job delivering newspapers. Since his mom worked at the university, he delivered a paper to her his friends into the club.

Unfortunately, the college-aged students were not thrilled to have a 14-year-old-kid training with them, given the nature of their vigorous workouts and especially the sparring matches. Jeff Smith was not only able to keep up with the older students but he became just as tough and strong as the best of them. By the time he became a brown belt, he had served as the head instructor for the club. In 1968, he received his black belt and continued teaching for two more years.

By 1970, Jhoon Rhee asked Smith to teach at his school in Washington. In time, Smith became part of the trio of advocates for the art. They included himself, Allen Steen, and J. Pat Burleson.

The 1970s proved to be huge decade for Smith as he began to test his skills on the open Karate tournament circuit as a point fighter. Keep in mind,

point fighting in those early days was more like semi-contact, so broken ribs were commonplace.

In only a few short years, Smith became one of the top fighters on the circuit. He was such an imposing force that he beat some of the greatest competitors of that era, including Howard Jackson, Darnell Garcia, Bill Wallace, John Natividad, and many more.

The 1970s also introduced a new form of fighting called Full-Contact Karate. It was a match to the knockout, and only a handful of point fighters were able to make the transition into this new sport, and Jeff Smith was one of them.

In 1974, Smith stepped into the ring and stepped into history by becoming the first Professional Karate Association (PKA) World Light Heavyweight Kickboxing Champion. He continued fighting for another decade with a 21-7 record.

A Man Without Limits
Chuck Sullivan

Chuck Sullivan

BORN
November 13, 1932

BIRTHPLACE
Chicago,
Illinois
USA

PRIMARY STYLE
American Kenpo

Chuck Sullivan is a man of many talents and several historical accomplishments. He was only the third person in history to receive a black belt awarded by Ed Parker. He played a key role in developing the Long Beach International Karate Championships. He was the first to put provide long-distance Kenpo training, and he was the first to showcase the martial arts in sculpture.

Sullivan had been an avid student of Ed Parker, the founder of American Kenpo Karate, for many years when Parker informed him that he would be testing for this black belt. Sullivan disagreed but said he was not ready. Parker

said, "It's not your decision to make; it's mine." So, on Sept 17, 1962, Sullivan took his first step into history by becoming one of the first to be awarded a black belt under Ed Parker.

American Kenpo was still relatively new to the martial arts world, and with one school, it would be a challenge to get the word out. Sullivan, however, had an exciting idea. He recommended recording the entire Kenpo system on 8mm training films. Through this, they could enlighten future students about the system and hopefully put a little money in their pocket.

Delighted with the idea, Parker said he would do all the training, but it was up to him to do all the directing, editing, packaging, advertising, and distribution, with the proceeds going 50/50. So, 8mm film training was born for Kenpo, and Sullivan took another leap into history. Close to two decades later, videos were invented, and Sullivan converted them all for a new market.

A year later, in 1963, Karate tournaments started to spring up across the country. Although Karate wasn't part of the American landscape until the mid-1940s, it had enough followers to start hosting competitions. Ed Parker felt that to bring additional attention to American Kenpo, he would

host a similar event. To conduct a little research, Parker attended every single tournament examining their methods and execution.

Looking for advice from his innovative student, Chuck Sullivan, together they would map out the tournament right on Parker's dining room table. From ring sizes to judges to awards, Sullivan assisted his instructor and played a key role in hosting the 1964 Long Beach International Karate Championships.

Although they only expected it to be a small event, it became more than they could imagine. Two years later, Sullivan became the tournament's director.

In his spare time, Sullivan was a creative artist. He would often work with clay sculpting simple bits of pottery. One day, Sullivan felt that the martial arts was not represented artistically anywhere. So, he thought it would be nice if they could hire a professional sculptor to capture the image of Ed Parker.

When the artist completed his work, it was beautiful, but it looked like a posed figure. There was no essence, no movement; it didn't capture the spirit of Kenpo. Though only an amateur, Sullivan felt that because he was a Kenpo stylist, he would be better suited for capturing what Kenpo really means. So, after a few years of trial and error, Kenpo sculptures were created.

When Sullivan decided to go on his own, he felt it was important to carry on the spirit of Ed Parker to a new generation. Sullivan fondly recalls, "When I met Parker, he was a huge Hawaiian fellow, and every time he moved, the ground seemed to shake."

Steve Sanders was one of Sullivan's early students who became one of the most recognized fighters in history.

陳觀泰飾演大刀王五，是一位氣度非凡的京師大俠士，豪勇愛人。
Chen Kuan-tai plays chivalrous swordsman, Wang Wu.

Film Warrior and Real Life Champion
Chen Kwan Tai

Chen Kwan Tai

BORN
September 24, 1945

BIRTHPLACE
Guandong Province
CHINA

PRIMARY STYLE
Monkey Kung Fu
(Tai Shing Pek Kwar)

It was the Shaw Bros., a Hong Kong film company, that dominated the world. It all began with the release of "Five Fingers of Death," starring Lo Wei. It was so successful that it created the Kung Fu movie boom of the 1970s.

It was the classic Chinese period pieces that captivated American audiences. Although the films were sometimes translated into English, the Chinese actors became household names. They included Alexander Fu Sheng, David Cheung, Ti Lung, Chi Quan Chun, and most notably, Chen Kwan Tai.

Chen Kwan Tai was different than all the rest. He was slightly older and appeared more mature. He would often be cast as the big brother of the clan. He was strong, and his Kung Fu skills were unmatched. His most famous film was his role in the "Flying Guillotine," but he did so many other great ones.

Chen Kwan Tai began his acting career in his first film, "Draschen" in 1969. For the next few years, he was cast in various roles but only in small parts. It was then Shaw Bros. director Chang Cheh discovered him. This was 1972 as the Kung Fu movie boom was about to hit, and the Shaw Brothers needed great talent.

Not only was he an accomplished actor, but what sold the studio on

investing in Chen Kwan Tai was that he was an accomplished martial arts practitioner, a master of Kung Fu. A senior student of icon Chan Sau Chung, Chen was also a Kickboxing champion who was once the Light Heavyweight Champion of Southeast Asia. He was one of the few Shaw Bros. actors that were actual martial artists.

He was immediately cast in the leading role in "The Boxer from Shan-

tung," followed by the "Four Riders" and "The Water Margin" all in 1972. From that point on, Chen Kwan Tai was featured in a number of co-starring roles with the biggest stars of the Shaw Bros. line-up.

His popularity continued to increase through his films like "The Tea House" and "Big Brother Cheng," both directed by Chih Hung Kwei. After the untimely death of Alexander Fu Sheng in 1983, one of his primary co-stars and the darling of the Shaw Bros. films, it was up to Chen Kwan Tai to carry on the torch for the Kung Fu movies.

A former fireman, Chen Kwan Tai has starred in over 150 films, 80 of them with the Shaw Brothers. He branched out to other productions companies of which he was both the director and the star, this being the 1977 film

"Iron Monkey."

Playing the good guy hero was most of his roles, but as he got a little older, he took on a few bad guy character roles, such as the boss in "Crippled Avengers."

Chen Kwan Tai has never stopped acting. In 2006, he appeared in Wilson Yip's martial arts fantasy, "Dragon Tiger Gate," and in 2012, "The Man with the Iron Fists," and in 2018, "Keyboard Warriors."

Chen Kwan Tai was one of the most recognized and respected actors in the Hong Kong movie genre. He brought real martial arts into the lineup, which dramatically impacted his fellow co-stars and raised the bar in martial arts stuntfighting.

The Dragon of Chinese Kung Fu
James Wing Woo

James Wing Woo

BORN
September 26, 1922

DIED
August 27, 2014

BIRTHPLACE
Oleum,
California
USA

PRIMARY STYLE
Shaolin
Kung Fu

James Wing Woo was born in 1922. His father had a restaurant on the property of the Standard Oil Refinery up North in Oleum, California, and it was right there, in the restaurant, that James was born as the second of eight boys.

When James was six years old, his father had gotten himself involved in the Tong Wars. The Tongs were considered the Chinese mafia at the time for some reason; his father had a price on his head, so they decided to pack up their bag and move back to their homeland, China.

The Woo family settled in Canton. It was the capitol of Kwantung province and was located on the southern part of China. It was there that

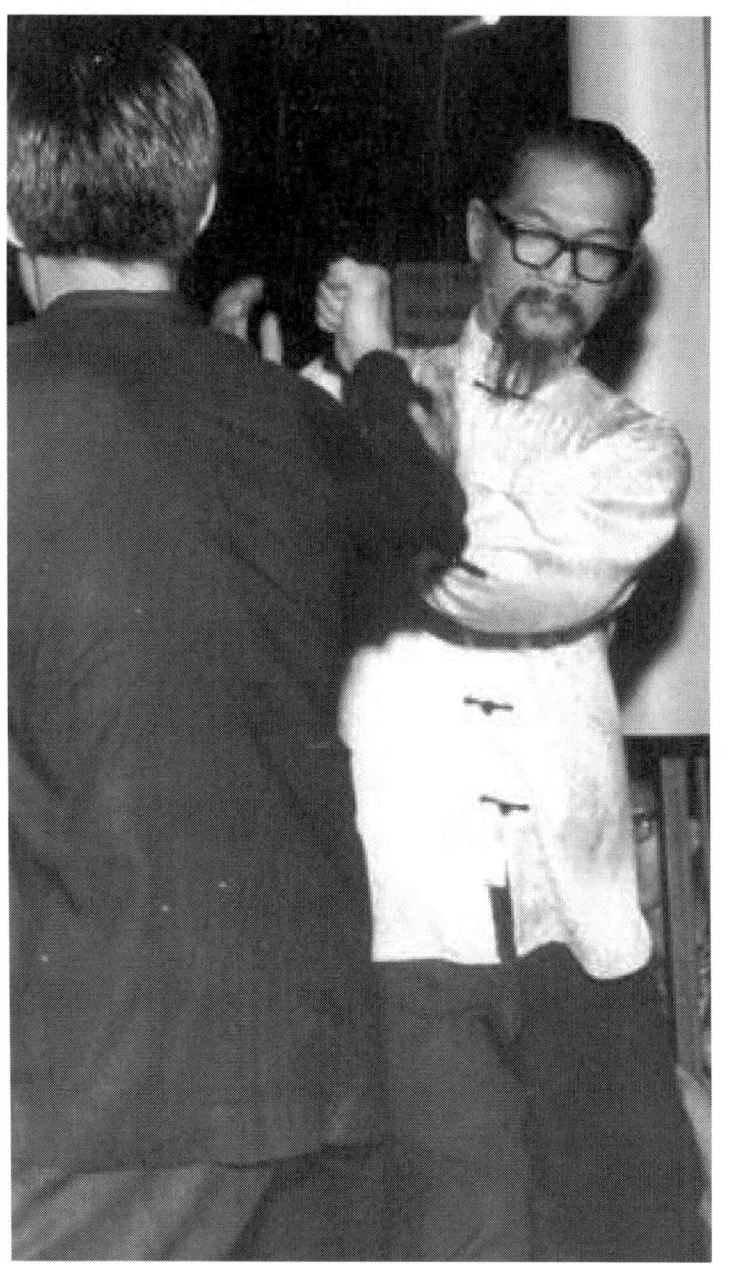

James Wing Woo started his journey in the martial arts. First, he began learning Tai Chi from his godfather. Then, friends from school started teaching him some movements in Kung Fu.

A year later, in 1929, Japan began invading Northern China, and many of the martial arts instructors packed up their bags and moved to Canton. For James, now 12, he allowed him to learn a variety of Shaolin styles.

As Japanese troops were getting closer to Canton, the Woo family decided that splitting up would be the easiest thing to do. Some stayed a little longer while others went to Kowloon, and the remainder fled to

California.

James ended up with one of his brothers settling in San Francisco. Now 16, he took a job as a waiter while still going to school. The year was 1938.

Now James Wing Woo continued practicing the Kung Fu he learned and it came in handy at the restaurant when someone took a swing at him. He blocked it and hit the guy hard, knocking him down.

Woo seemed prone to fight as he moved from restaurant to restaurant, getting fired because of fighting.

Woo decided to enlist in the military as a cook. One day, while on shore

patrol on Treasure Island near San Francisco, he saw this couple fighting and tried to break it up. The guy's beautiful girlfriend rewarded him with a smack on the face.

    Many years later, he was introduced to a young lady by a friend. He looked at her, and it was the same girl who had hit him back on Treasure Island. The two started going to gather and later got married.

After his discharge from the Navy, he began studying Kung Fu under a friend of his father who was part of the Hop Sing Tong; his name was Lau Bun. Lau was a highly respected individual and one of the top Choy Li Fut Kung Fu teachers in the world. It was there that Woo would build his foundation.

One day, while working out in the park, he met a group of American Kenpo Karate artists visiting from Los Angeles, CA. After developing a friendship, James Wing Woo and a group of Lau Bun's students went to visit their school in Pasadena, CA. The school was run by the founder of American Kenpo, Ed Parker.

Woo moved down to Los Angeles, and he and Parker quickly developed a friendship. For many years, they shared ideas, techniques, and methods to help improve each other's skills. They even wrote a book together called "The Secrets of Chinese Karate." At the Pasadena studio, Woo also taught a class on Kung Fu to many of Parker's black belts.

Something happened, and there was a disagreement, and Woo decided to return home to San Francisco, but several of the higher-ranked students asked him to remain. He agreed, and in 1961, he opened the Academy of Karate Kung Fu with many of Parker's students deciding to stay with Woo.

A unique individual, James Wing Woo was one of those early Kung Fu pioneers that would teach anyone willing to learn.

"2014 Funakoshi Award Winner"

The Father of Manga and Anime
Osamu Tezuka

Osamu Tezuka

BORN
November 3, 1928

DIED
February 9, 1989

BIRTHPLACE
Toyonaka,
Osaka
JAPAN

Osamu Tezuka was chosen to be the 2014 winner of the "Funakoshi Award." Named after Gichin Funakoshi for his countless contributions to the martial arts. He was not a martial artist, but he dramatically impacted the martial arts world.

Tezuka was an artist in the areas of manga and anime. Manga, which means drawing on paper, and anime, which means cartoon animation, were invented long before him, but Tezuka revolutionized its style and incorporated life stories.

Using a multitude of angles and different points of view, he was able to bring more depth,

meaning, and emotion to his characters. It was a process that would later be part of every manga and anime artist would include.

Revered as the "Walt Disney of Japan," Osamu was able to change the face of literature and influence a new generation. He had a natural story-telling ability and was extremely passionate about his work. He had a pioneering spirit and believed his experiences underdone during the war played an influential role in his life.

Sporting an odd-looking black French beret, he wore thick-rimmed

glasses topped off with a 24-hour smile. He was born in Osaka, Japan, in 1928 and attended the University to become a physician, which he did.

Being a doctor, however, wasn't his passion, and even though he was fully licensed, he said his sights on the make-believe world of anime and manga. Tezuka noted that Walt Disney's animated film "Snow White" had a tremendous influence on his life. He knew one day he would be just like Walt Disney.

His dreams were fulfilled as he was referred to by many as the called the "Father of Anime and Manga."

Tezuka made an immeasurable impact on the world with more than 700 manga titles with 150,000 pages, all drawn by hand. He had more than 60 anime titles and was considered the greatest manga creator in history.

A working artist throughout his life, his most famous work began in the 1960s with the introduction of the manga "Astro Boy," which he later adapted into one of the first successful Japanese anime. This was immediately followed by "Kimba, The White Lion."

Although he was only 60 when he passed, Tezuka was able to change the landscape of both Japanese and American animation single-handedly.

PHOTOGRAPHERS

Sean O.S. Barley
Jeff Berting
Black Belt magazine
Richard Bustillo
Brett Churchill
Doug Churchill
Fighting Stars
George Foon
Getty Photos
Keith Barraclough
Duke Tirschel
Steve Escarcega
Karate Illustrated
Kick Illustrated
Ed Ikuta
Inside Kung Fu
Kono Magazine
Buck Sam Kong
Rod Kuratomi
Bruce Lee Foundation
Beverly Lucaylucay
Ma-mags.com
Martialinfo.com
MAsuccess
Martial Arts Movies
Brian Matsuda
Michael Matsuda
Ed Parker Jr.
Mario Prado
Warner Bros.
Douglas Lim Wong
Keith Yates
Associated Press
Jim Coleman
Robert Young

It's so important that amazing individuals like those portrayed in this book are remembered. Our goal was to provide at least five pictures that would serve to portray a span of the lifetime of an individual. For the most part, we felt that we have accomplished that. However, in some cases it was difficult to not only find the photograph, but find the photographers in order to give them proper credit. If anyone should come across a photograph you would like to contribute or a missed photo credit and want it included, please let us know.

INDEX LISTING

Ahn, Philip, 228
Blanks, Billy, 159
Bustillo, Richard, 209
Cagney, James, 26
Caldwell, Linda, 260
Camacho, Art, 30
Canete, Cacoy, 212
Carradine, David, 153, 234
Chan, Sau Chung, 240,
Chat, Mike, 34
Chi, Kuan-Chiun, 136
Chiang, David, 138, 139, 286, 287
Choi, Yong Sul, 56
Chong, Jun, 98
Cook, Keith, 150
Corcoran, John, 8, 265
Cunningham, Peter, 172
DePasquale Jr, Michael, 180, 183
Dietrich, Marlene, 229
Dillard, Mike, 24

Dye, David, 204, 207
Emperado, Adriano, 40
Esquivel, Sal, 222
Fleishman, Eric, 159
Forbach, Gary, 42, 151
Ford, William Chris, 205
Fu Sheng, Alexander, 134, 285
Fukudo, Keiko, 104
Garcia, Darnell, 225
Goldberg, Alan, 178
Greenberg, Marlene, 157
Hackleman, John, 267
Han, Bong Soo, 63
Harrison, Kayla, 110
Hayakawa, Sessue, 227
Hong, James, 184
In, Hyuk Suh, 82
Iwamatsu, Mako, 191
Jackson, Howard, 275
Jae, Ji-Han, 52
Johnson, Dave, 196

Johnson, Dwayne, 130
Johnson, Otto, 204
Kahana, Kim, 23
Kaihewalu, Sol, 204, 207, 222
Kane, Robin, 253
Kano, Jigoro, 109
Katz, Tim, 260
Kee, Hwang, 46
Ken, Tak Hoi, 243
King, Larry, 268
Kong, Buck Sam, 63
Lau, Bun, 166
Laughlin, Tom, 27, 58
LeBell, Gene, 22
Lee, Bruce, 54, 286
Lee, Taejoon, 116
Lefiti, Haumea, 222
Lem, Jerry, 246
Lem, John 246, 247
Lewis, Joe, 273
Leong, Al, 252

302

INDEX LISTING

Lewis, Charles, 258
Liddell, Chuck, 264
Lung, Ti, 28, 139, 287
Manu, Michelle, 159
Macchio, Ralph, 31
Marolt, John, 222
Marquez, Frank, 206
Marquez, Manuel, 155
Matsuda, Karen, 95
McCarthy, Paul, 244
McQueen, Steve, 191
Morita, Pat, 31
Nai, Khanom Tom, 140
Natividad, John, 225
Novak, Al, 64
Nunez, Richard, 207, 222
Ohshima, Tsutumo, 122
Okamura, Gerald, 203, 257
Ortiz, Tito, 266
Parker, Ed, 225, 279. 280
Piscopo, Joe, 183
Primicias, Frank, 246
Rabago, Richard, 202
Rhee, Phillip, 100, 101
Rhee, Simon, 100, 101, 103
Roiles, Kenneth, 211, 213
Roiles, Francis, 211, 213
Roiles, Felix, 208
Roiles, Tanya, 211
Rothrock, Cynthia, 30
Salinas, Alex, 211
Severn, Dan, 70
Shamrock, Ken, 128
Shuey, Mark, 214
Shum, Leung, 76
Silliphant, Stirling, 13
Smith, Jeff, 270
Steen, Alan, 274
Stone, Mike, 223
Sullivan, Chuck, 276
Tabura, Ted, 204
Tai, Chen Kwan, 137, 138, 282
Takeuchi, Todd, 253
Talamantes, Jess, 159
Tezuka, Osamu, 294
Togisala, Butch, 205
Tom, Michael, 253
Totton, Carl, 88
Tuiolosega, Tino, 220
Tung, Roger, 146
Urquidez, Benny, 12
Vitali, Keith, 24, 274
Wallace, Bill, 273
Waggle, Justin, 92
Woo, James Wing, 288
Wong, Anna May, 226
Wong, Ark Y., 90
Wong, Carrie Ogawa, 41
Wong, Doc Fai, 167
Wong, Doug, 41, 68, 69, 90, 151, 253, 255
Wong, Raymond, 246
Wong, Y.C., 246
Yuen, Kam, 15

Made in the USA
Columbia, SC
10 July 2022